AROMA & OLIVE OIL

AROMA & OLIVE OIL: THE ESSENTIALS OF HEALTHY & DELICIOUS CUISINE
by Micki Sannar

Copyright © 2012 Micki's Kitchen

Published in the United States by
Mikko International, LLC
Highland, Utah 84003

Sannar, Micki
Aroma & Olive Oil: The Essentials of Healthy & Delicious Cuisine / by Micki Sannar
p. cm.
Includes bibliographical references and index.

ISBN-13: 978-0-9801349-2-6
ISBN-10: 0-9801349-2-7
First Printing: August 2012

1. Cooking 2. Health I. Sannar, Micki II. Title

10 9 8 7 6 5 4 3 2 1

Editor: Dena Ming-Hall
Cover and Book Designer: Julie Arnold
Photographer/Food Stylist: Micki Sannar
Image Specialist: Wesley Lovick
Contributing Writers: Dave Sannar, Estelle Werve and Kalli Wilson

The dōTERRA name is a trademark used under license from
dōTERRA International, LLC of Orem, Utah. www.doterra.com

To order additional copies, visit the author's website at www.aromaandoliveoil.com.
Also visit: www.oliveoildesserts.com, www.facebook.com/aromaoliveoil
Email: micki@aromaandoliveoil.com, Twitter: @oliveoilchic

Aroma & Olive Oil

THE ESSENTIALS OF HEALTHY & DELICIOUS CUISINE

by Micki Sannar

Table of Contents

RESOURCES

APPETIZERS

DRINKS

MAIN DISHES

SIDE DISHES

SOUPS

DESSERTS

ACKNOWLEDGEMENTS

Writing a new cookbook is like going on a treasure hunt; always seeking to find what has never been found. For me, writing *Aroma & Olive Oil* is that adventure; only I believe that I have found a treasure in blending my two favorite oils on earth, Olive Oil and Essential Oil.

This labor of love would not have been possible without many who patiently encouraged me to complete this, the first ever, healthy pairing of Olive Oil and therapeutic grade Essential Oils... all wrapped up in one delicious cookbook.

A special thank you to dear my friends Kalli & John, who I blame as the inspiration behind this cookbook. Without them I would have never written these recipes. To Emily who turned up the heat by opening a challenge to me in a small window of time. To Dena, my amazingly beautiful and talented editor who stepped right in and worked alongside me every step of the way, as well as working long hours into the night. To Suzanne, Cydne, Michelle, Kristi Lani, Kathleen, Leah, Ranae, Terri, Brenda, Kalli, Rindee, Lillian, and Kristen, my Angel recipe testers, who helped insure the taste and accuracy in each recipe. I am more grateful to you then you can ever imagine.

To Julie, my designer who pulled off the impossible, you are amazing!

To my darling David, my husband and the love of my life, for supporting me in everything I do and showing me that I can reach beyond what I think, and holding my hand through it all. I love you always. To my 4 beautiful children, Ryan, Chris, Mikey, and Jessi who have patiently tasted just about everything I have created & offered me their advice, which I truly value. To my Mama, who always supports me in everything I do, and my Daddy-o, who taught me from a very young age how to step way out of the box. You really did unleash some creative... okay, weird... concepts, in combining unlikely ingredients and making food taste delicious, most of the time.

Last, but most certainly not least, my gratitude for my Father in Heaven whom I am never afraid to acknowledge. You always give me exactly what I need, you even put salt in my cookies when I forget. You are the ultimate inspiration behind everything I do that is good in my life. I am thankful forever, for all you have given me.

You are all a treasure and a blessing in my life, and for that I am truly appreciative.

~ Micki Sannar

PREFACE

Preparing scrumptious meals is all about family and friends. There is joy found in cooking with and for others.

My Philosophy on Wealth:

When I have enough food to feed myself,
I am doing somewhat well.
When I have enough to feed my family,
I am well off.
When I have enough food to feed others,
especially those who come to my home,
I AM WEALTHY!

Since writing my first cookbook *Olive Oil Desserts*, I have continued to find methods of improving the foods I prepare for my family and friends. My dear friend Kalli, who is an expert when it comes to Essential Oils, challenged me to write some recipes using CPTG Essential Oils. That is where the fun and the questions began.

Because Essential Oils can become fragile when exposed to heat, and Olive Oil is fairly resistant to heat, I wondered what would happen if I combined the two oils? I needed a method to preserve the life enhancing, therapeutic benefits found in both the Extra Virgin Olive Oil and Essential Oils when cooking. Would the efficacy of the Essential Oils be preserved at higher temperatures if blended with Olive Oil? After numerous tests, I discovered that the answer is yes! I am excited to share these methods with you, my family and friends.

I hope you enjoy my recipes as much as I have enjoyed creating and eating them. Some of them may sound a little different at first—give them a try! I think you will discover the blending of deliciously intense flavors will excite your taste buds, and perhaps invite you to share them with family and friends.

I truly believe that delicious and healthy foods benefit us the most when shared with someone we love.

I hope you become very wealthy!

A BRIEF HISTORY OF TWO MIRACULOUS OILS

What was once a great part of our ancestor's existence still lives on today with the many life giving and healing benefits found in both Essential and Extra Virgin Olive Oils.

ESSENTIAL OIL

As you embark on a more virtuous culinary path and unleash the power of Essential Oils in your kitchen, you should know that these oils have ancient roots. Essential Oils have been used for thousands of years for their healing properties. Ancient Egyptian hieroglyphs, Chinese writings, and Biblical texts unveil the extensive use of Essential Oils in food preparation as medicine, for beautification, and for religious purposes.

Anciently, Essential Oils were highly prized & considered more valuable than gold.

In modern times, the French chemist, Rene-Maurice Gattefosse, revived the use of Essential Oils for therapeutic purposes when he healed a badly burnt hand with pure lavender oil. His research was also furthered by colleague Dr. Jean Valnet who used Essential Oils to treat wounded soldiers during World War II with amazing success. The therapeutic use of Essential Oils keeps gaining popularity as scientific research findings support the countless health benefits of Essential Oils that come from plants—some maybe even growing in your own backyard.

EXTRA VIRGIN OLIVE OIL

One of the world's oldest known cultivated trees is the olive tree. Native to southern Asia Minor, the tree quickly spread across the Mediterranean seaboard over 6000 years ago. Due to the food and medicinal qualities of the fruit, it was not long before the olive and its distinctive oil became a highly valued and important part of civilization.

Homer called Olive Oil "liquid gold." In Israel, King David ordered guards to watch over Israel's olive groves to ensure their safety. The Egyptian, Phoenician, Greek, and Roman civilizations all helped spread the olive throughout the Mediterranean region.

Anciently, Olive Oil was used for cooking, fuel, commerce, light, religious rituals, and medicine. The Greek physician Hippocrates referred to Olive Oil as "the great therapeutic."

Today you can find olive trees and their life giving oil, all over the world, with many of the world's finest olives being grown, pressed into Extra Virgin Olive Oil, bottled, and sold right in our own back yard. From California to Texas, olive trees are dotting the American landscape as a symbol of health and vitality.

11

ABOUT ESSENTIAL OILS

Who does not love the smell of a fragrant rose blooming on a warm summer morning, or the scent left lingering after peeling an orange? And what is about the heavenly aroma that fills a home when cinnamon rolls are baking in the oven? Most of the lovely fragrances we experience in life originate from plants, which have even more to offer than just delighting our sense of smell.

Essential Oils are the natural aromatic nutrients extracted from the bark, seeds, stems, roots, flowers, and leaves of various plants. These plants contain hundreds of highly concentrated diverse biological material with therapeutic value. Because these life giving oils have a small molecular structure and are fat soluble, they are naturally and easily absorbed into the body delivering therapeutic benefits.

Although there are several different extraction processes used today, the preferred method to obtain the most pure Essential Oils is by distillation or cold pressing.

COLD PRESSING

This technique is reserved typically for Essential Oils. Produced from citrus rinds where the oils are expressed mechanically, similar to Olive Oil extraction. The process involves slightly warming the rinds (no higher than 120°F), and applying extreme pressure which separates the water from the natural oil essence. The water is discarded and the oil is placed in climate controlled conditions. Prior to the discovery of steam distiillation, all Essential Oils were extracted through cold pressing.

STEAM DISTILLATION

Herbs and other plant material such as those noted on this page are placed in a large tank and then steam is introduced into the lower section of the tank. The steam passes through the plant material, naturally extracting the volatile plant compounds by combining with them and transforming into a condensed liquid. The liquid is directly transferred into another tank. The water and Essential Oil in the condensed liquid naturally separates and the oil is placed in climate controlled conditions.

Pure Essential Oils are the essence of the living plant, beautifully condensed in a bottle. To protect the life giving property of the plant essence, it is imperative that the correct extraction process is utilized under exacting laboratory conditions to produce therapeutic grade oil.

To distinguish pure therapeutic grade oil from imposter oils you need only view, smell, and feel the texture of the oil. A pure oil is clean and clear, with a balanced aroma profile; never overbearing in any one scent note. The texture is not oily and absorbs quickly into the skin.

Using Essential Oils in food is an exciting and delicious way to enjoy the natural therapeutic benefits of the oils.

ABOUT OLIVE OIL

Although the traditional olive press is still used by some Olive Oil producers around the world, the Decanter Centrifuge is the most wildly used extraction method in the Olive Oil industry today. Olives are crushed into a fine paste that is then stirred, releasing the nutritionally dense enzymes locked inside. The paste is then spun, causing the oil to separate out creating the most aromatic, medicinally beneficial Extra Virgin Olive Oil available today.

With over a thousand varieties of olives, and more blends of Olive Oil, it is good to taste a few types of Extra Virgin Olive Oil to see which varieties you like best. Most major cities have specialty stores where you can sample Olive Oil. I encourage you to visit, taste, and learn more about this amazing liquid gold.

CLASSIFICATIONS OF CONSUMABLE OLIVE OIL

- *Extra Virgin Olive Oil:* First pressing of the olives, contains no more than 0.8% acidity, most flavorful, no defects, no filler oils, and no chemical refining. Highest nutritional value; oleic acids, polyphenols, Omega-3, 6, & 9.

- *Virgin Olive Oil:* Second pressing with acidity less than 2%, flavorful, no filler oils, and no chemical refining. High nutritional value.

- *Pure Olive Oil:* A Blend of refined Olive Oil and either Extra Virgin or Virgin Olive Oil. Little taste. Nutritional value.

- *Olive Oil:* A blend of virgin oil and refined oil, may have defects, flavorless, often little nutritional value.

- *Olive Pomace Oil:* A blend of refined Olive Oil and Virgin Olive Oil. Rarely sold at retailers, used by many restaurant chains in certain foods. There is usually no nutritional value.

EXTRA VIRGIN OLIVE OIL FOR BAKING

Abrosana, Arbequina, Hojiblanca, Picual, and Picuda oils generally have a very mild flavor and work well for baking tasty desserts.

LOOK FOR THESE IDENTIFIERS WHEN PURCHASING OIL

- Harvest date and location

- Labeled "cold pressed"

- Bottled in dark colored glass

- Sold by reputable sources, such as specialty markets.

STORAGE

Extra Virgin Olive Oil will typically remain fresh without refrigeration for 6 to 9 months. Remember to store it in a cool dark place, as exposing Olive Oil to continued heat, oxygen, or light, causes it to deteriorate.

THE BREAKTHROUGH: ESSENTIAL & OLIVE OIL BLENDS

With each original recipe my ultimate goal is to deliver an exceptionally flavorful and healthful dining experience.

Traditionally, the method of cooking with strongly flavored Essential Oils was to dip a toothpick in the Essential Oil, and then to stir the toothpick in the recipe to add flavor to the dish. This method still works for some recipes, but with varied results. I have developed a new, innovative method that delivers more accurately the full benefits of Essential Oils into the foods you cook.

The challenge with using Essential Oils in cooking is the efficacy of the oils diminishes as they are heated. As the temperature rises the oils begin to break down. Additionally, during the heating process Essential Oils are susceptible to a "smoking point" where the oils begin to deteriorate. At this point the value of the oils is reduced or completely lost.

After extensive testing and experimentation, I have recently discovered a method for protecting the efficacy of Essential Oils in cooking.

The solution is the right blend of Extra Virgin Olive Oil and Essential Oils.

Authentic Extra Virgin Olive Oil has a smoke point average of 395°F and most Essential Oils have smoke points within the range of 110°F to 215°F. The smoke point will vary depending upon the types of oil being used. While testing the smoke points of my Essential Oils and Extra Virgin Olive Oil blends I discovered the smoke points of the blends were raised significantly.

Therefore, when you create and use Essential Oil/EVOO blends, you increase the smoke point of the Essential Oils sufficient to allow the therapeutic benefits of the oils to be present in prepared foods.

Extra Virgin Olive Oil is the perfect carrier oil for use in cooking and baking as it provides both the heart health benefits found in EVOO and the healing properties found in Essential Oils while controlling the oil's strong flavors.

You can find my Essential and Olive Oil Blend recipes on page 114.

COOKING WITH OLIVE OIL & ESSENTIAL OILS

Cooking and Baking with Olive Oil and Essential Oils is all about enjoying the delicious flavor and unique therapeutic benefits found only in the essence of a living plant.

Having Essential Oils in your culinary arsenal means you will have many delightful flavors at your fingertips and the confidence in knowing you are preparing healing foods for your family and friends.

Only use certified pure therapeutic grade oils when you cook. A list identifying Essential Oils which are generally recognized as safe (GRAS) by the FDA is on page 119.

WHEN PREPARING FOOD WITH ESSENTIAL OILS:

- Always store foods prepared with Essential Oils in **glass** containers in the refrigerator. These oils are powerful!

- Essential Oils are vulnerable to heat, it is best to add them at the final stages of cooking, just prior to serving.

- Re-heating prepared or cooking food with pure Essential Oils in the microwave will render them therapeutically ineffective, so I would not recommend it.

- To insure the freshness of your Essential Oils, always store them in a cool, dark place.

- Oils such as Oregano, Basil, Thyme, Rosemary, Fennel, or Marjoram can pack as much power in just one drop as is found in 3 ounces of its dried herb. Just remember, when it comes to Essential Oils, less is more.

When unsure of how much Essential Oil to use in your own recipes, the best advice is to start small or use my Essential Oil/EVOO Blends found on page 114.

PAIRING ESSENTIAL OILS WITH FOODS:

- *Salad Dressings and Dipping Oils:* basil, clove, coriander, fennel, ginger, lavender, lemon, lime, tangerine, black pepper, rosemary, and thyme.

- *Meat Sauces:* use basil, fennel, ginger, lemon, lemongrass, lime, marjoram, pepper, rosemary, thyme, and wild orange.

- *Desserts and Baking:* use cinnamon, clove, coriander, ginger, grapefruit, lavender, lemon, peppermint, tangerine, and wild orange.

- *Herbal Teas:* use chamomile, cinnamon, ginger, lavender, lemon, peppermint, tangerine, and wild orange.

- *Refreshing Drinks:* use grapefruit, lavender, lemon, lime, peppermint, tangerine, and wild orange.

- *Flavored liquid sweetener:* use chamomile, cinnamon, clove, ginger, grapefruit, lavender, lemon, lime, tangerine, and wild orange.

HEALTH BENEFITS OF OLIVE OIL

Since ancient times, olives and olive oil have been used for food and to treat many different diseases and maladies. Hippocrates was one of the first medical practitioners to record the health and therapeutic benefits of Olive Oil. Modern science has validated these benefits and identified many more. Over the past few decades, many studies from researchers worldwide suggest that Olive Oil helps in the prevention of heart disease and cancer, promotes a healthy digestive system, reduces the effects of arthritis and offers protection against a host of other ailments.

HEART DISEASE

Studies show that a Mediterranean style diet greatly lowers the risk of cardiovascular disease.[1] Olive Oil high in phenolic content, has anti-inflammatory and anti-clotting properties which result in healthier blood vessels and reduced cardiovascular disease.[2] The US FDA suggests Olive Oil may reduce the risk of coronary heart disease.[3]

HIGH BLOOD PRESSURE

Olive Oil intake is inversely associated with both systolic and diastolic blood pressure.[4] Moderate intake of Olive Oil was successful in reducing the blood pressure of healthy men.5 Using extra virgin olive oil, patients were able to lower their antihypertensive medication.[6]

CHOLESTEROL

Olive Oil has been proven to lower low density lipoproteins (LDL) and raise high density lipoproteins (HDL), resulting in reduced chances of coronary heart disease.[7]

BREAST CANCER/CANCER

In a recent study conducted in Europe, phenols in olive oil have been demonstrated to reduce leukemia cells.[9] Drinking Olive Oil daily reduces oxidation damage to cells, a precursor to cancer.[10]

ARTHRITIS

A Mediterranean diet with most fat coming from olive oil results in a "reduction of inflammatory activity, an increase in physical function, and improved vitality" for patients with Rheumatoid Arthritis.[11]

CONCLUSION

The health benefits of Olive Oil have been proven repeatedly by scientists around the world. There are literally hundreds of scholarly research articles on the subject with only a small sampling included here. The irrefutable fact is simply that olive oil consumption makes you healthier and prevents disease. Please see references at the back of the book for more information.

THERAPEUTIC BENEFITS OF ESSENTIAL OILS

Therapeutic Essential Oils are made up of hundreds of different chemical constituents and contain regenerating, immune enhancing, oxygenating properties of plants. The unique mix of each pure Essential Oil's active ingredients determines how the oil can be used. Some oils are used to promote physical healing. Others may be used for their emotional value.[1]

Studies from various researchers worldwide provide insight into the therapeutic benefits of Essential Oils.

ANTIBACTERIAL

Numerous studies on the topical antibacterial effects of Essential Oils have found the oils to possess substantial antimicrobial activity.[2, 3]

ANTIFUNGAL

Certain Essential Oils are fungistatic and fungicidal.[4]

ANTISEPTIC

Some Essential Oils contain terpene citral, which is used to combat cold sores and the essential oil thymol has proven antiseptic properties.[5, 6]

EMOTIONAL

Lavender oil in particular has a significant sedative effect.[7] The effects of aromatherapy result from a direct pharmacological interaction rather than an indirect central nervous system relay.[8]

CONCLUSION

This constitutes only a very small sample of the research documenting the therapeutic benefits of Essential Oils. Please see references on page number 120 at the back of the book for more information.

DIETARY OPTIONS: YOU HAVE CHOICES

Because of the amazing flavor and health benefits found in both Olive Oil and Essential Oils, many of my recipes are naturally dairy-free, gluten-free, or vegan. Even though this cookbook is not based on any particular diet, I have implemented 3 icons as a guide to certain recipes which may accommodate your dietary choices.

G *Gluten-Free Icon* indicates recipes that do not contain wheat or other ingredients with gluten.

D *Dairy-Free Icon* indicates recipes that do not contain any dairy ingredients.

V *Vegan Icon* indicates recipes that do not contain any meat, dairy, or eggs.

CONVERSION AND SUBSTITUTIONS

For those of you who want to enjoy your favorite foods but find yourselves limited because of dietary restrictions, I have included conversion and substitution charts for your convenience. Try the substitutions to make the recipes in this cookbook vegan or try converting your own recipes.

CONVERTING YOUR DESSERTS WITH OLIVE OIL

- Converting to Olive Oil (page 115)
- Gluten Free Options (page 116)
- Egg Alternatives for Baking (page 118)
- Dairy Alternatives (page 117)

MIDDLE EASTERN TABOULI
WITH MINT ESSENCE
(page 28)

GREEN & RED MOJO PICON (pages 26-27)

Appetizers

BASIL & FENNEL BRUSCHETTA W/TOASTED SLICES Ⓓ|Ⓥ

An antipasto from Italy originating around the 15th century has come a long way. Aided by the healthful benefits found in Fennel and Basil Essential Oils, this tomato based appetizer is not only delicious; it may even provide a healthy enhancement to your diet.

PREPARATION: 10 minutes **COOK TIME:** 20 minutes **SERVES:** 10 to 12

1½ pounds ripe Plum, Cherub,
    or Cherry tomatoes, quartered
2 garlic cloves, minced
¼ cup Extra Virgin Olive Oil
1 teaspoon red wine vinegar
1 teaspoon Basil/EVOO Blend*
1 teaspoon Fennel/EVOO Blend*
1 teaspoon sea salt
½ teaspoon pepper
1 baguette French bread
    or similar Italian bread
Additional Extra Virgin Olive Oil,
    for brushing bread

* See page 114

1. Preheat oven to 425°F.

2. Combine the tomatoes, garlic, Olive Oil, vinegar, Basil and Fennel/EVOO Blends, salt and pepper in a large mixing bowl. Gently mix all of the ingredients and add additional salt, to taste.

3. Slice baguette about ½ inches apart. Coat one side of each slice with Olive Oil, and place on a baking sheet with the Olive Oil side up. Place in oven and Toast on the top rack until light brown. Turn the slices over and toast again.

4. Align the bread on a serving platter, Olive Oil side up. Spoon bruschetta on top and serve immediately.

MANGO & BLACK BEAN SALSA

Ⓖ|Ⓓ

Because of the powerful flavor in Lime and Coriander Oils this Black Bean Salsa comes alive with taste. Serve it up with your favorite tortilla chips and let's get this party started...

PREPARATION: 15 minutes   **COOK TIME:** 5 minutes   **SERVES:** 6 to 8

1 (15-ounce) canned black beans, drained
½ red bell pepper, diced small
½ green bell pepper, diced small
½ red onion, diced small
2 ripe mangoes, cubed small
2-3 drops dōTERRA Lime Essential Oil
1 drop dōTERRA Coriander Essential Oil
2 tablespoons Extra Virgin Olive Oil
¾ cup pineapple juice
2 tablespoons ground cumin
½ cup cilantro, chopped
1 tablespoon jalapeno pepper, finely chopped
1 teaspoon sea salt

1. In a medium size bowl, add beans, peppers, onions, and mangos.

2. In a small size bowl, add Lime and Coriander Oils, Olive Oil, juice, cumin, cilantro, jalapeno pepper, and salt; stir to combine.

3. Pour dressing over bean mixture and blend together. Serve cold with tortilla chips on the side.

The Mango tree plays a sacred role in India;
it is a symbol of love and some believe that
the Mango tree can grant wishes.

HONEY HUMMUS IN THYME

Ⓖ Ⓓ Ⓥ

Any time is a good time for this Hummus in Thyme.
I love hummus any time, and that is all I have to say this time.

PREPARATION: 15 minutes   **SERVES:** 8 to 10

½ cup Extra Virgin Olive Oil
½-¾ cup fresh lemon juice
1 teaspoon honey
6 small garlic cloves, peeled
3 drops dōTERRA Lemon Essential Oil
1-2 drops dōTERRA Thyme Essential Oil
1 drop dōTERRA Black Pepper Essential Oil
1 (15-ounce) can garbanzo beans, drained
1 (15-ounce) can northern white beans, drained
1 teaspoon sea salt

1. Place all of the ingredients into a blender. Or for a thicker, chunkier hummus, use a food processor and blend until mixture reaches desired smoothness.

2. Taste and add more salt as needed.

3. For a thinner hummus use more lemon juice and Olive Oil.

4. Serve with warm pita bread.

GREEN MOJO PICON

G | D | V

Originating from the Canary Islands, this flavorful and versatile sauce is full of green power. The Lemon Essential Oil in this delicious Picon offers a mood elevator that will keep you happy from the very first taste. Use it as a dressing, meat topping, bread dip, or anything you would like to turn up the flavor up on.

PREPARATION: 15 minutes   **SERVES:** 6 to 8

½ cup Extra Virgin Olive Oil
1 teaspoon sea salt
½ teaspoon white pepper
3 drops dōTERRA Lemon Essential Oil
2 teaspoons red wine vinegar
2-4 garlic cloves
1 bunch parsley
½ bunch cilantro

1. Place Olive Oil, salt, pepper, Lemon Oil, vinegar, and garlic in blender. Blend until liquefied.

2. Slowly add parsley and cilantro; blend until smooth.

3. Enjoy it as a salad dressing, dipping sauce, or meat and vegetable dressing.

RED MOJO PICON

D | V

Enjoy the new taste of a red pepper that was brought over to the Canary Islands from Spain. Re-created by everyone who prepares this mojo sauce it is said that there are as many versions as there are stars in the sky.

PREPARATION: 15 minutes   **SERVES:** 8 to 10

4 peppers, red, bell or any other non-spicy red pepper

½ small red onion

3-4 garlic cloves, peeled

½ teaspoon ground cumin

1 teaspoon red pepper flakes

2 drops dōTERRA Lemon Essential Oil

1 drop dōTERRA Lime Essential Oil

1½ teaspoons sea salt

½ teaspoon black pepper

1 cup Extra Virgin Olive Oil

1-2 slices stale white bread, crusts trimmed if very dry

¼ cup water* or chicken broth

Red vinegar

* For Vegan preparation use water

1. Place peppers, onion, garlic, cumin, hot pepper flakes, Lemon Oil, Lime Oil, and salt & pepper in a blender or a food processor. Blend mixture to the consistency of a paste.

2. While blending, drizzle in the Olive Oil gradually. Alternately add small pieces of the bread and small amounts of water or broth until the sauce is slightly thickened. Slowly add the vinegar, according to your desired taste. Enjoy with potatoes, meat or fish.

Featured on previous page with Green Mojo Picon.

MIDDLE EASTERN TABOULI WITH MINT ESSENCE Ⓓ Ⓥ

Also known as Tabbouleh, this Lebanese favorite is often viewed as a pathway to better health. Packed with nutrients and Essential Oils, this delicious starter will have you well on your way down that path.

PREPARATION: 30 minutes   **SERVES:** 8 to 10

2 cups cracked wheat

2 cups very hot water

1 cucumber, finely chopped

2 medium tomatoes, finely chopped

1 bunch green onions, about 8 thinly sliced

2 cups fresh parsley, chopped

1 garlic clove, minced (optional)

DRESSING

1-2 drops dōTERRA Lemon Essential Oil

1 drop dōTERRA Peppermint Essential Oil

1 drop dōTERRA Black Pepper Essential Oil

½ cup fresh lemon juice

¾ cup Extra Virgin Olive Oil

2 teaspoons sea salt, or to taste

1. Soak the cracked wheat in hot water until the water is absorbed, about 30 minutes. When ready, drain and squeeze out any excess water.

2. Place prepared vegetables and cracked wheat in a large salad bowl, and mix to combine.

3. In a small mixing bowl, blend dressing ingredients and pour over vegetable mixture. Mix until combined. Serve chilled.

MIDDLE EASTERN
TABOULI WITH
MINT ESSENCE

PEA PESTO WITH LEMON & GARLIC (G)

If you enjoy the sweet and fresh taste of peas, the deep flavor of Basil, and the rich pungency found in fresh garlic; then you may be eating this starter well into the dinner hour.

PREPARATION: 10 minutes   **SERVES:** 8

2 cups frozen peas
¼ cup grated Parmesan cheese
4 garlic cloves, minced
5 drops dōTERRA Lemon Essential Oil
2 teaspoons Basil/EVOO Blend*
¼ cup Extra Virgin Olive Oil
1 teaspoon sea salt
Ground black pepper

 * See page 114

1. Place all of the ingredients in a blender and pulse until combined.

2. Turn the blender and mix on a medium speed for another 30 seconds.

3. Serve with warm, soft pita bread or over slices of garlic toast.

PEPPER JACK BEAN DIP WITH CORIANDER & LIME Ⓖ

This is the perfect appetizer to serve at your next get together. With a delicious southwestern flavor, combined with the added benefits found in the Essential Oils, your guests will never know they are eating something good for them.

PREPARATION: 10 minutes   **COOK TIME:** 25 minutes   **SERVES:** 8

1 (15-ounce) can black beans, drained and rinsed
1 teaspoon Extra Virgin Olive Oil
½ cup onion, chopped
2 garlic cloves, minced
½ cup fresh or frozen corn kernels
¾ cup tomatoes, chopped
½ cup mild picante sauce
1 teaspoon ground cumin
1 drop dōTERRA Coriander Essential Oil
1 drop dōTERRA Lime Essential Oil
1 teaspoon chili powder
½ cup Pepper Jack cheese, shredded
Lime slices and cilantro, for garnish

1. Place half of the black beans in a food processor or mash by hand.

2. In a large skillet, heat Olive Oil on medium-high. Stir in onion and garlic; and sauté for about 5 minutes.

3. Add mashed and remaining beans, corn, tomatoes, picante sauce, cumin, Coriander & Lime Oils, and chili powder. Blend the mixture together, and cook for 3 minutes or until hot.

4. Remove from heat, place in serving bowl and immediately stir in cheese. Garnish and serve warm with tortilla chips.

NON-ALCOHOLIC ZESTY CITRUS
& RASPBERRY SANGRIA (page 45)

STRAWBERRY & BASIL
LEMONADE (page 42)

Drinks

APPLE LIME RICKEY

A new twist on an old favorite; this little sipper delivers a powerful yet soothing taste. With the zingy flavor of Lime and the fizz of Sparkling Cider you will feel like little angels are dancing on your taste buds.

PREPARATION: 5 minutes   **SERVES:** 6

32 ounces Concord grape juice
16 ounces sparkling apple cider
 4 drops dōTERRA Lime Essential Oil
Lime slices, for garnish

1. Add all ingredients into a large glass pitcher and stir. Serve over ice cubes. Garnish and enjoy!!!

VANILLA GINGER ALE WITH AGAVE

Originating during the 1840's in England, Ginger Ale was intended to be for stomach ailments. But the taste caught on and it soon became a huge sensation. This Ginger Ale is truly refreshing and helpful for an upset stomach or just any time you want a soothing and delicious drink.

PREPARATION: 5 minutes   **COOK TIME:** 5 minutes   **SERVES:** 1

 1 (12-ounce) glass sparkling water
2-4 tablespoons Agave Nectar
 ½ teaspoons pure vanilla extract
 2 drops dōTERRA Ginger Essential Oil
Ice cubes
 1 lime, sliced

1. Add the sparkling water, Agave, vanilla and Ginger Oil into a 16-ounce glass, and stir it until the Agave is completely dissolved.

2. Add ice cubes. Garnish and enjoy!!!

CITRUS & LAVENDER SPRITZER OVER COCONUT ICE (G)(D)(V)

A fruity and refreshing thirst quencher with the subtle essence of Lavender, this slightly fizzy spritzer will leave you relaxed and ready to enjoy the remainder of even the most hectic of days.

PREPARATION: 10 minutes   **SERVES:** 2

- 1 cup sparkling water
- 1 cup coconut water, chilled
- 2-4 tablespoons Agave Nectar
- ½ cup fresh lemon juice
- ¼ cup fresh lime juice
- 1-2 drops dōTERRA Lavender Essential Oil
- 1 drop dōTERRA Lemon Essential Oil
- 1-2 cups coconut ice (below)

Slice of lemon and/or lime, for garnish

1. Add water, coconut water, Agave, and lemon & lime juices into a small pitcher; and stir to combine.

2. Add Lavender and Lemon Oils; give the mixture a quick stir, and serve it over coconut ice cubes. Garnish and enjoy!

COCONUT ICE

1. Pour coconut juice into an ice tray and place in the freezer overnight.

CHOCOLATE EXTREME PEPPERMINT FRAPPE

The deep taste of chocolate in this tantalizing Frappe is the perfect night cap for you and your sweetheart. With the lovely fresh essence in Peppermint Essential Oil, you are instantly ready for that good night kiss.

PREPARATION: 10 minutes   **SERVES:** 4

> 1 pint frozen chocolate yogurt or low-fat ice-cream
> 2 cups cold milk
> ¼ cup chocolate syrup
> 1-2 drops dōTERRA Peppermint Essential Oil
> ½ cup ice cubes

Peppermint sprigs, for garnish

1. Place the frozen yogurt, ice, milk, chocolate syrup, Peppermint Oil into a blender.

2. Blend on high speed until smooth. Garnish and serve immediately.

HOT CRANBERRY & MANDARIN CIDER

(G) | (D) | (V)

This quick and simple hot beverage delivers a spicy blend of flavors in a warm and inviting cup of antioxidant goodness. With the power of Cinnamon, Clove, Ginger, Bergamot, and Lime Essential Oils, you will enjoy the full bodied flavor of warm cider while filling your home with holiday essence

PREPARATION: 15 minutes **COOK TIME:** 15 minutes **SERVES:** 8 to 10

1 large can mandarin oranges, with juice

1 large can pineapple, sliced

1 can frozen apple juice, prepared

1 can of frozen cranberry apple juice, prepared

¼ cup Agave Nectar syrup, honey, or cane sugar (optional)

2 teaspoons pure vanilla extract

½ lemon, sliced

4-6 drops dōTERRA Cinnamon Essential Oil

2 drops dōTERRA Clove Essential Oil

3 drops dōTERRA Ginger Essential Oil

2 drops dōTERRA Lime Essential Oil

1 drop dōTERRA Bergamot Essential Oil

1. Combine mandarin oranges and pineapple slices in a blender. Cover and mix on high speed for 15 to 20 seconds, until smooth.

2. Pour the mixture into a large pot and add prepared juice. Bring mixture to a complete boil for about one minute. Reduce heat to low; add Agave, vanilla, and lemon slices; simmer for about 5 minutes.

3. Remove from heat and add the Cinnamon, Clove, Ginger, Lime & Bergamot Essential Oils. Give it a quick stir and enjoy!

Interesting fact: Bergamot essence offers many health benefits, but the actual orange looking fruit is not known to be edible.

THE EZ GREEN SMOOTHIE

G | D | V

For those of us whose family will sometimes refuse to eat their veggies; don't get mean, go Green! One sip and it won't be difficult to charm them all with this deceptively delicious Green Smoothie. With a touch of Lime and Tangerine Essential Oils, a powerful, healthy day awaits you.

PREPARATION: 5 minutes   **SERVES:** 2

½ cup white grape juice
½ apple, peeled
½ cup pineapple
1 cup green grapes
½ ripe banana, peeled
1 teaspoon Agave Nectar (optional)
2 drops dōTERRA Lemon Essential Oil
3-4 drop dōTERRA Tangerine Essential Oil*
A small sliver of lime
1 teaspoon pure vanilla extract
1 cup ice cubes
2 cups fresh spinach

* Substitute Wild Orange Essential Oil if Tangerine Oil
  is unavailable

1. Place all of the ingredients in order into a blender. (If you have a wimpy blender, you may have to run this a couple of times.)

2. Start your mixer on a lower speed and gradually increase, or if you have a smoothie button, go for it!

3. Blend it until completely combined and enjoy the delicious healthiness!!!

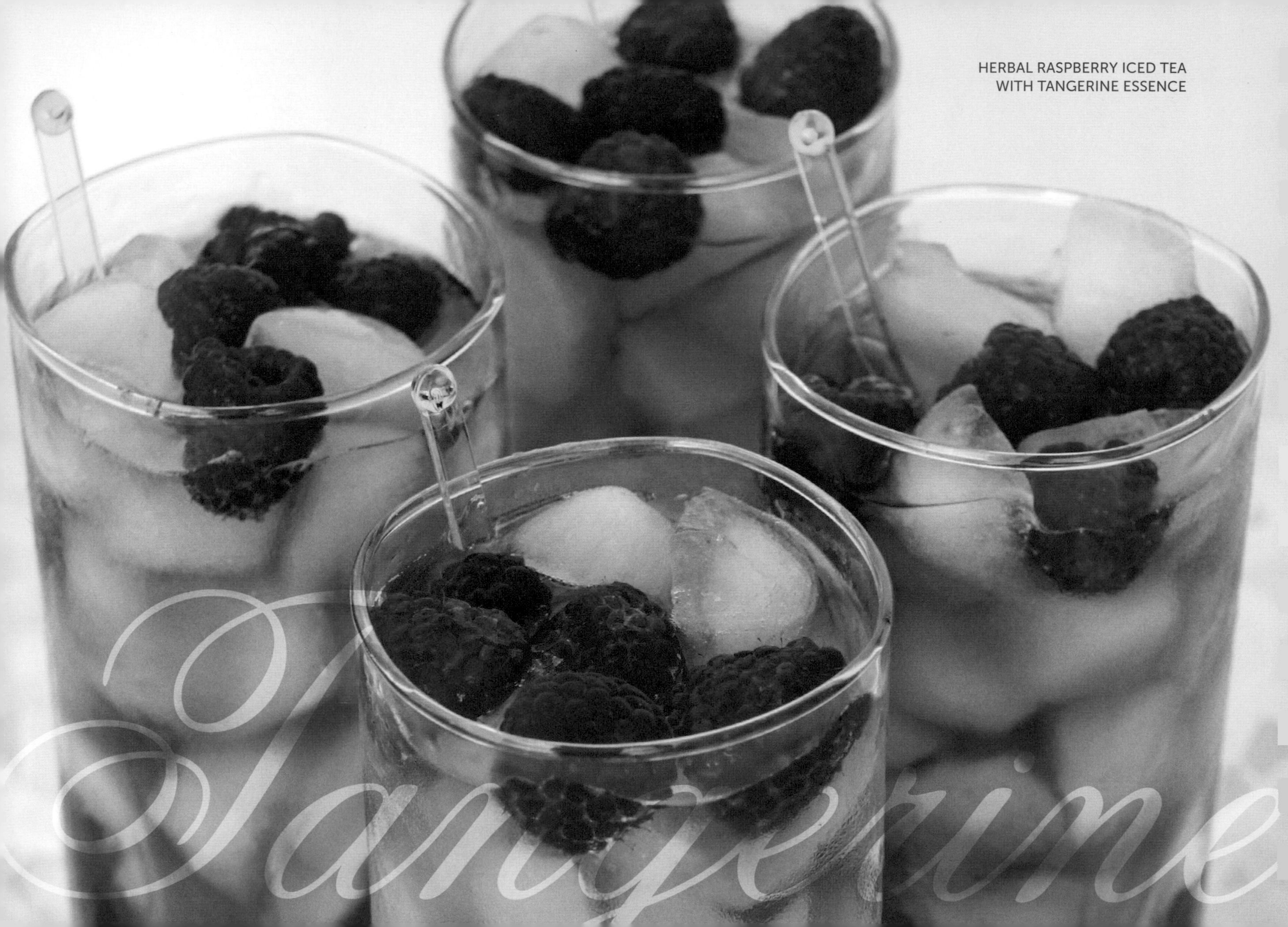

HERBAL RASPBERRY ICED TEA
WITH TANGERINE ESSENCE

HERBAL RASPBERRY ICED TEA
WITH TANGERINE ESSENCE

(G) (D) (V)

A great alternative for unhealthy soft drinks; this blend of herbal tea, infused with citrus Essential Oils, fruit juice, and a hint of the cool mint found in Bergamot Essential Oils is so invigorating you will have a hard time putting it down after only one sip.

PREPARATION: 5 minutes   **COOK TIME:** 15 minutes   **SERVES:** 4 to 6

    6   cups water
    3   drops dōTERRA Tangerine Essential Oil*
    1   drop dōTERRA Grapefruit Essential Oil
    1   drop dōTERRA Bergamot Essential Oil
    5   raspberry herbal tea bags
 1½   cups pomegranate juice
  ⅓   cup Agave Nectar

Raspberries and tangerine or orange slices, for garnish

* Substitute Wild Orange Essential Oil if Tangerine Oil is unavailable

1. Add the water into a large pot and bring to a boil. Add tea bags and remove from heat; cover and allow to steep for 15 minutes.

2. Discard tea bags; add Agave and mix until dissolved. Add pomegranate juice & Tangerine Oil; stir, and serve over ice cubes. Garnish and enjoy!!!

You can never get a cup of tea large enough or a book long enough to suit me.

~ C. S. Lewis

STRABERRY & BASIL LEMONADE

Ⓖ Ⓓ Ⓥ

An herbaceous addition on a hot day; this unusual blend of strawberries, lemon, and a hint of basil essence will titillate the taste buds. This healthful thirst-quencher will be a pleasant surprise from the very first sip.

PREPARATION: 5 minutes   **SERVES:** 4 to 6

24 ounces water
½ cup cane sugar
3 cups frozen strawberries
8 drops dōTERRA Lemon Essential Oil
2 lemons, juiced
¼ cup Basil water
Ice cubes
Basil and lemon slices, for garnish

BASIL WATER

1 cup water
1 drop dōTERRA Basil Essential Oil

1. Place water and sugar in a blender and process on high speed, until sugar is dissolved.

2. Add strawberries, Lemon Oil, lemon juice, and Basil water; mix on high speed until completely combined. Serve over ice cubes. Garnish and enjoy!!!

BASIL WATER

1. Place the water and Basil Oil into a glass jar and mix together. Cover and store in the refrigerator until ready to use.

The Greek word for Basil is Βασιλεύς, *meaning: Royal Remedy.*

STRAWBERRY &
BASIL LEMONADE

ROMANTIC VANILLA & HONEY LEMONADE

This spicy lemonade contains Vanilla, Cinnamon, and Ginger which are all associated with putting you in the mood for love. You make the lemonade and whatever happens after that is nobody's business.

PREPARATION: 15 minutes   **COOK TIME:** 5 minutes   **SERVES:** 6 to 8

1   cup cane sugar

¼   cup honey

1   cup water, plus more

1   teaspoon pure vanilla extract,
    or ½ of a vanilla bean pod*

1½ cups freshly squeezed lemon juice
    (about 12 lemons)

1   drop dōTERRA Lemon Essential Oil

2   drops dōTERRA Cinnamon Essential Oil

1   drop dōTERRA Ginger Essential Oil

Lemon wedges, for garnish

1. In a medium size pot combine the sugar, honey, and 1 cup of water and place it on medium to high heat. If using a ½ vanilla bean pod* or vanilla extract, add to honey water mixture.

2. Bring mixture to a boil and cook for 3 to 5 minutes, or until sugar is completely dissolved. Remove from heat, and allow to cool.

3. Place fresh lemon juice into a pitcher, and remove the vanilla bean pod from syrup mixture.

4. Add syrup mixture into the lemon juice and add enough water to equal 1 gallon of lemonade. Stir in the Lemon, Cinnamon and Ginger Oils until mixed.

5. Serve over ice cubes. Garnish and enjoy!!!

* Cut vanilla bean in ½ lengthwise using the back of a knife and scrape the vanilla seeds from the pod. Add the seeds and the pod to the pot.

NON-ALCOHOLIC ZESTY CITRUS & RASPBERRY SANGRIA

G D V

PREPARATION: 10 minutes   **SERVES:** 8 to 10

1 large lemon, peeled and chopped

1 fresh lime, peeled and chopped

2 cups fresh or frozen raspberries

1 orange, peeled and chopped

¼ cup Agave Nectar

2 cups 100% pure cran-raspberry juice

2 cups 100% Concord grape juice

1 cup fresh squeezed orange juice

4-6 drops dōTERRA Lemon Essential Oil

1-2 drops dōTERRA Lime Essential Oil

2 drops dōTERRA Tangerine
or Wild Orange Essential Oil

1-2 drops dōTERRA Peppermint
Essential Oil

4 cups sparkling mineral water

Citrus slices and fresh mint leaves,
for garnish

1. Place all fruit in a blender or food processor and pulse 5 or 6 times until partially chopped.

2. Transfer to a punch bowl, and stir in Agave Nectar, fruit juices, and Essential Oils.

3. Place punch bowl in the refrigerator and chill for at least 3 hours, allowing the flavors to infuse.

4. Right before serving, stir in the sparkling water and serve over ice. Garnish and serve.

VEGETARIAN TOSTADAS
(page 62)

LEMON CHICKEN TENDERS & PENNE PASTA (page 56)

Main Dishes

BALSAMIC & ROSEMARY RIBEYE STEAK WITH LIME HORSERADISH SAUCE

This tender and flavorful Steak combined with Rosemary and Lime Essential Oils is a family favorite. So, when we are craving something juicy and tender, that is when it is time to fire up the grill!

PREPARATION: 15 minutes   **COOK TIME:** 25 minutes   **SERVES:** 4

4 (1-pound) Ribeye Steaks, bones removed
1 teaspoon Rosemary/EVOO Blend*
3 tablespoons Extra Virgin Olive Oil
2 drops dōTERRA Lime Essential Oil
3 tablespoons balsamic vinegar
1 tablespoon sea salt
1 tablespoon freshly ground black pepper
Lime wedges, for garnish

SAUCE

½ cup mayonnaise
2 tablespoons bottled horseradish
2 drops dōTERRA Lime Essential Oil
⅛ teaspoon white pepper, or to taste

* See page 114

1. Remove steaks from refrigerator, and place on the counter for about 1 hour.

2. Combine Rosemary/EVOO Blend, Olive Oil, Lime Oil, and vinegar.

3. Brush the steaks evenly on both sides with mixture and sprinkle with salt and pepper, and set it aside for 30 minutes to 1 hour.

4. Place each steak onto preheated grill, and cook for 2 to 3 minutes. Turn the steaks 90 degrees and grill another 2 to 3 minutes, producing cross grill marks, repeating the process on both sides. Remove from the grill and slice steaks across the grain. Garnish and serve with Lime Horseradish Sauce on the side.

SAUCE

1. In a bowl blend together sauce ingredients; cover and chill.

BALSAMIC & ROSEMARY
RIBEYE STEAK WITH LIME
HORSERADISH SAUCE

BEAN BURGERS WITH LIME YOGURT SAUCE

If you want to eat something delectably healthy and different, say Hola to this meatless burger with a Mexican twist. It will excite your senses especially if you put a few drops of habanero sauce on top.

PREPARATION: 30 minutes   **COOK TIME:** 7 to 10 minutes   **SERVES:** 6

2 (15-ounce) cans black beans, or pinto beans, drained

½cup chopped red onion

1 small can mild green chili peppers, chopped

2 cups dry breadcrumbs

¾cup bottled chunky salsa

3 large eggs

2 teaspoons ground cumin

1 teaspoon sea salt

Extra Virgin Olive Oil

6 whole wheat hamburger buns, toasted

SAUCE

2 cups plain Greek yogurt

1 cup finely diced cucumber, peeled

1 cup chopped fresh cilantro

2 drops dōTERRA Lime Essential Oil

Sea salt and pepper, to taste

1. Place beans in a food processor or mash by hand.

2. In a medium size bowl, add beans, onion, chilies, breadcrumbs, 2 tablespoons salsa, eggs, cumin, and salt. Blend mixture, and shape into 6 patties.

3. Heat 2 to 3 tablespoons of Olive Oil in a large skillet; add patties and cook for 3 to 5 minutes per side, or until heated through. Place on toasted buns and top with yogurt sauce and salsa.

SAUCE

1. Combine all ingredients and top black bean burgers.

MARJORAM CHICKEN BREASTS W/DILLY LEMON SAUCE Ⓖ

A member of the mint family, Marjoram was known to the Greeks and Romans to hold the essence of happiness. If that is truly the case, you will be ecstatic after trying this savory dish.

PREPARATION: 10 minutes   **COOK TIME:** 25 minutes   SERVES: 6

6 boneless, skinless chicken breast, tenderized to ¼-inch
2 tablespoons Extra Virgin Olive Oil, divided
4 drops dōTERRA Lemon Essential Oil
1 tablespoon Marjoram/EVOO Blend*
½ teaspoon freshly ground black pepper

SAUCE

¾ cup light sour cream
¾ cup yogurt
2 drops dōTERRA Lemon Essential Oil
½ teaspoon sea salt
2 tablespoons fresh dill, chopped
¼ cup scallions, finely chopped

* See page 114

1. In a medium size bowl, combine 1 tablespoon Olive Oil, Lemon Oil, Marjoram/EVOO Blend, and pepper. Place in a re-sealable plastic bag and add the chicken. Stir to coat, and marinate in the refrigerator for at least one hour, preferably longer if possible.

2. Heat remaining Olive Oil on medium in a large skillet. Add chicken, and sauté for 4 to 6 minutes on each side, or until cooked through.

SAUCE

1. Combine sour cream, yogurt, Lemon Essential Oil, salt, dill, and scallions. Drop a dollop over chicken and serve over a bed of your favorite rice.

CARIBBEAN SHRIMP WITH WARM PINEAPPLE SALSA Ⓖ | Ⓓ

Invite the tropics into your kitchen with this wonderfully appetizing dish. Served over a bed of Coconut and Lime Rice, this Island delight is sure to have you planning your next vacation to the Caribbean islands!

PREPARATION: 20 minutes   **COOK TIME:** 15 minutes   **SERVES:** 4 to 6

1   garlic clove, finely minced

1   teaspoon Rosemary/EVOO Blend*

1   teaspoon Thyme/EVOO Blend*

¼   teaspoon each black pepper, sea salt and cayenne pepper (omit for mild flavor)

1   pound jumbo shrimp, peeled and deveined with tails

1   tablespoon Extra Virgin Olive Oil

Lime slices, for garnish

SALSA

2   tablespoons Extra Virgin Olive Oil

1½   sweet onion, chopped

1   teaspoon curry powder

24   ounces pineapple tidbits, drained

1½   tablespoons cider vinegar

1   teaspoon sea salt

2   tablespoons honey

2-3   drops dōTERRA Wild Orange Essential Oil

* See page 114

1. Combine all of the ingredients except Olive Oil and marinate for 1 to 2 hours.

2. About 20 minutes before cooking shrimp, prepare Warm Pineapple Salsa, and set aside.

3. Heat 1 tbsp Olive Oil in a large skillet, on med-high.

4. Add shrimp mixture and cook for 2-4 min per side.

5. Remove the Shrimp from skillet, top it with Warm Pineapple Salsa, garnish and serve immediately.

SALSA

1. Heat Olive Oil in a large skillet on medium-high, add onions, and cook until tender and translucent.

2. Stir in curry powder, pineapple, vinegar, salt, and honey; bring mixture to a light boil. Immediately reduce heat and simmer for 10 minutes. Remove from stove, add Orange Oil and serve over Shrimp.

CARIBBEAN SHRIMP WITH WARM PINEAPPLE SALSA
AND DOUBLE COCONUT LIME RICE *(page 70)*

COCONUT CHICKEN CURRY

COCONUT CHICKEN CURRY

G | D

This creamy and savory coconut milk-based curry is full of flavor and exotic spice. The rich and delightful taste and healing power found in Ginger and Coriander Essential Oils will have planning to make this dish again very soon.

PREPARATION: 15 minutes   **COOK TIME:** 25 minutes   **SERVES:** 4 to 6

½ cup whole unsalted cashews
1 pound skinless, boneless chicken thighs, cut into 1-inch pieces
1½ teaspoons sea salt
4 tablespoons Extra Virgin Olive Oil, divided
1 medium onion, thinly sliced
2 garlic cloves, minced
¼ cup coconut, finely shredded
1 (14-ounce) can unsweetened coconut milk
¼ cup frozen peas
1 tablespoon curry powder
1 teaspoon cumin
¼ teaspoon mustard powder
1 drop dōTERRA Ginger Essential Oil
1 drop dōTERRA Coriander Essential Oil
2 tablespoons cilantro, chopped

1. Preheat oven to 350°F, and spread cashews into a small baking pan and bake for 5 minutes, or until lightly toasted. Remove from oven and set aside.

2. Season chicken with salt and heat 3 tablespoons of Olive Oil in a large skillet on medium. Add chicken and sauté until golden brown on both sides. Remove chicken onto a plate and let cool.

3. In the same skillet heat remaining Olive Oil and add onion and garlic. Sauté until onion is translucent, and add coconut to sauté for another 2 to 3 minutes.

4. Stir in coconut milk and peas. Bring it to a light boil, and reduce heat to low. Blend in the curry, cumin, and mustard powder, and remove from heat. Stir in chicken and Essential Oils, and simmer for 5 minutes. Transfer to a serving bowl and top with cilantro and cashews.

LEMON CHICKEN TENDERS & PENNE PASTA

Garlic and Lemon Essential Oil bring out the intense flavor of this tender chicken and pasta dish. Paired with a light salad and a slice of bread, this is a meal your family will savor.

PREPARATION: 15 minutes   **COOK TIME:** 20 minutes   **SERVES:** 6

1 (12-ounce) package penne pasta
3 tablespoons Extra Virgin Olive Oil
3 pounds chicken tenders,
  each piece cut into thirds
8 green onions, sliced
1 large garlic clove, minced
6 tablespoons butter
6 tablespoons all-purpose flour
¼ teaspoon chili powder
2½ cups chicken broth
¾ cup non-fat milk
1 tablespoon Dijon mustard
5 drops dōTERRA Lemon Essential Oil
1 drop dōTERRA Coriander Essential Oil
¾ teaspoon sea salt
½ teaspoon pepper

1. Prepare the penne pasta according to the package directions, place in a large bowl and set aside.

2. In a large skillet, heat Olive Oil on high; add chicken pieces and sauté for 5 to 8 minutes. Add green onions and garlic; sauté for another 3 minutes. Remove from heat and pour chicken mixture over cooked pasta.

3. In the same skillet, melt butter and stir in flour and chili powder to form a paste. Over a medium heat, add broth and milk, and continue stirring soup until thick and bubbly.

4. Stir in the mustard, Lemon and Coriander Oils, salt and pepper. Simmer 3 to 5 minutes, or until thickened. Combine with pasta and chicken. Serve hot.

LEMON CHICKEN TENDERS & PENNE PASTA

SLOW COOKED SAVORY SALMON

Ⓖ|Ⓓ

A touch of Thyme and Lemon Essential Oils bring out a delightful flavor in this slowly baked, moist and delicious salmon filet. It may take a little extra time, but the savory flavor & tender goodness are certainly worth waiting for.

PREPARATION: 15 minutes   **COOK TIME:** 25 minutes   **SERVES:** 4

2 tablespoons Extra Virgin Olive Oil, divided
4 (6- to 8-ounces) boneless salmon fillets, skin on
1 tablespoon Thyme / EVOO Blend (see page 114)
3 drops dōTERRA Lemon Essential Oil
Zest of 1 lemon
Sea salt
Freshly ground black pepper
4 lemon wedges, for serving

1. Preheat oven to 275°F and line a rimmed baking sheet with aluminum foil. Brush ½ tablespoon of Olive Oil on foil. Place salmon fillets, skin side down; set aside.

2. Mix the remaining Olive Oil, Thyme / EVOO Blend, Lemon Essential Oil, and lemon zest in a small bowl. Spread mixture over the salmon fillets, dividing equally. Season with salt and pepper, and let stand 10 minutes to allow flavors to marinate.

3. Bake salmon uncovered for 20 to 25 minutes, or until just opaque in center. Garnish and serve.

SOY SHRIMP WITH SCALLIONS & GINGER AIOLI Ⓖ

This tantalizing shrimp dish will be one meal to repeat for family and guests alike. With the essence of Ginger Essential Oil laced into a divine and delicious sauce, you will soon discover why this tasty shrimp does not last long at the dinner table.

PREPARATION: 30 minutes   **COOK TIME:** 20 minutes   **SERVES:** 6

¾ cup soy sauce

4 green onions, chopped

½ cup Extra Virgin Olive Oil

3 tablespoons unseasoned rice vinegar

3 tablespoons rice cooking wine (optional)

1½ tablespoons golden brown sugar

5 garlic cloves, chopped

36 large shrimp (about 1½-pounds), peeled and deveined

6 servings steamed white rice, prepared

AIOLI
Ginger Aioli

1 cup mayonnaise

2-3 drops dōTERRA Ginger Essential Oil

1. In a medium bowl, combine the soy sauce, green onions, Olive Oil, vinegar, sake, brown sugar, and garlic. Whisk marinade to blend. Add shrimp and toss to coat. Cover and refrigerate for 30 to 60 minutes, turning shrimp occasionally.

2. In a small bowl, combine mayonnaise and Ginger Oil. Place in the refrigerator.

3. Drain the marinade from the shrimp into a small saucepan, and bring to a low boil. Blend 2 tablespoons of marinade into the ginger aioli, while reserving the remaining marinade.

4. In a large skillet, heat remaining ¼ cup Olive Oil on medium. Add shrimp and sauté for 3 to 4 minutes.

5. Mound rice in the center of a large serving plate. Arrange the shrimp around rice, drizzle with aioli, and serve with reserved marinade.

WILD ORANGE & GRAPEFRUIT SOY GLAZED SALMON,
POTATO MASHERS WITH LEMON & PARSLEY *(page 76)*
AND LEMON THYME GARLIC SNAP PEAS *(page 72)*

WILD ORANGE AND GRAPEFRUIT
SOY GLAZED SALMON   Ⓖ Ⓓ

Simplicity is the key to preparing this divine citrus infused salmon. A dish that is as pretty as it is delicious will have your guests thinking that they have just been treated to a high end meal. Make it for dinner or anytime you are in the mood for something special.

PREPARATION: 10 minutes　　　**COOK TIME:** 45 minutes　　　**SERVES:** 6 to 8

¼ cup honey
¼ cup soy sauce
3 tablespoons fresh orange juice
4 drops dōTERRA Wild Orange Essential Oil
2-3 drop dōTERRA Grapefruit Essential Oil
2 tablespoons water
1 teaspoon honey Dijon mustard
2 tablespoons Extra Virgin Olive Oil
4 small salmon fillets, skin removed

1. In a small bowl, whisk together the honey, soy sauce, orange juice, Wild Orange Oil and Grapefruit Oil, water, and mustard; set aside.

2. Heat Olive Oil in a large skillet on medium until hot but not smoking. Cook salmon 2 to 3 minutes on each side, or until it is golden and just cooked through. Remove salmon.

3. Add honey mixture into the skillet and simmer on low, stirring occasionally, until it reaches a glaze-like consistency.

4. Pour glaze over salmon and serve warm.

VEGETARIAN TOSTADAS

G

You do not need to be a vegetarian to enjoy the delightful and filling taste of my delicious Veggie Tostadas. With the hint of Lime and Coriander Essential Oils, the healthy twist on an old family favorite will have you filled and satisfied after your first tostada, but don't stop there...

PREPARATION: 40 minutes **COOK TIME:** 35 minutes **SERVES:** 4 to 6

TOSTADAS

Corn tortillas

4 tablespoons Extra Virgin Olive Oil, divided

Sea salt

3 cups fresh or frozen corn

1 sweet onion, finely minced and divided

1 small red pepper, seeded and diced

1 small green pepper, seeded and diced

1-2 garlic cloves, minced

3-4 drops dōTERRA Lime Essential Oil

1 drop dōTERRA Coriander Essential Oil

CARNE ASADA SEASONING

White pepper

½ Bunch cilantro leaves, chopped

2 drops dōTERRA Lime Essential Oil

3-4 baked potatoes, skins removed and cubed

2 ripe avocados, sliced

½ head cabbage, thinly sliced

2-3 Roma tomatoes, diced

Lime wedges, for garnish

1. Heat oven to 400°F. Using 2 tablespoons of Olive Oil, brush 6 tostadas on both sides and sprinkle with salt. Place on a large baking sheet and heat for 5 to 8 minutes or until slightly crisp. Remove them from the oven and cool.

2. In a large skillet, heat the remaining Olive Oil on medium-high. Add half of the onion, and red and green peppers, and fry until mixture begins to brown; about 10 to 15 minutes.

3. Stir in minced garlic, Lime and Coriander Oils. Begin adding Asada seasoning and white pepper, to taste.

4. In a small bowl, mix remaining half minced onion, cilantro, and Lime Essential Oil together.

5. Starting with a corn tortilla on the bottom, place a spoonful of potatoes, sliced avocados, corn mixture, cabbage, and cilantro mixture. Top with tomatoes and garnish with ¼ wedge of lime.

VEGGIE SANDWICH WITH
GARLIC BASIL MAYONNAISE

VEGGIE SANDWICH WITH GARLIC BASIL MAYONNAISE

Where's the meat? Who cares? When you sink your teeth into this delicious Veggie Sandwich, you won't miss the meat for one moment.

PREPARATION: 15 minutes   **SERVES:** 2

2 teaspoons mayonnaise
1 teaspoon Basil / EVOO Blend*
1 small garlic clove, crushed
1 pinch of sea salt
4 slices whole wheat bread, lightly toasted
4 slices Cheddar cheese
2 slices red onion
¼ cup ripe olives, sliced and drained
1 small tomato, sliced
1 cucumber, sliced
1 medium ripe avocado, sliced
Romaine Lettuce
Sea salt and pepper, to taste
Your favorite Italian salad dressing

* See page 114

1. Combine mayonnaise, Basil / EVOO Blend, garlic, and salt in a small bowl. Spread over bread slices and layer with cheese, onion, olives, tomato, cucumber, avocado, and lettuce. Sprinkle with pepper.

2. Drizzle Italian dressing on each sandwich, slice and serve.

VIVACIOUS VEGAN CHILI

Ⓖ|Ⓓ|Ⓥ

This Vegan Chili serves up a fiber rich blend of beans, tomatoes, spices, and numerous Essential Oils making this vegan chili a perfect choice for a cold winter night. Serve it with cornbread or just a few crackers, either way you are sure to enjoy this filling and heartwarming meal.

PREPARATION: 25 minutes   **COOK TIME:** 60 minutes   **SERVES:** 8 to 10

2 tablespoons Extra Virgin Olive Oil

½ medium onion, chopped

2 bay leaves

1 teaspoon ground cumin

¼ cup chili powder

1 tablespoon sea salt

2 stalks celery, chopped

2 green bell peppers, chopped

1-2 jalapeno peppers, chopped

2 (4-ounce) cans green chili peppers, chopped and drained

3 garlic cloves, chopped

1 (28-ounce) can whole peeled tomatoes, crushed

4 Roma tomatoes, chopped

1 (15-ounce) can each kidney beans, black beans and whole kernel corn, garbanzo beans, drained

1 drop each dōTERRA Coriander, Thyme and Oregano Essential Oils, and Black Pepper Oil

1 avocado, sliced

Cilantro sprigs, for garnish

1. In a large pot, heat Olive Oil on medium-high. Add onion, bay leaves, cumin, chili powder, and salt. Sauté until onion is tender.

2. Add the celery, bell peppers, jalapeno peppers, chili peppers, and garlic and continue to sauté. When the vegetables are heated through, reduce the heat to low, cover, and simmer 5 minutes.

3. Add tomatoes, beans, and corn. Bring to a boil, cover and reduce heat to low, simmering for 45 minutes. Stir in all Essential Oils and simmer for 5 minutes. Remove from heat, garnish and enjoy!

YOGURT MARINATED CHICKEN W/PARSLEY MINT SAUCE Ⓖ

If you are looking for a fast, healthful, and flavorful meal for your family, this Yogurt Chicken is a fantastic choice. Start the marinade in the morning, then pop it out, and whip it up in no time for dinner. This entrée is not only quick and simple to prepare but it is splendidly delicious.

PREPARATION: 15 minutes   **COOK TIME:** 15 minutes   **SERVES:** 4

1 cup plain low-fat or non-fat yogurt

1 tablespoon Extra Virgin Olive Oil

2 teaspoons cumin

2 drops dōTERRA Lemon Essential Oil

2 garlic cloves, crushed

1 drop dōTERRA Coriander Essential Oil

4 boneless, skinless chicken breasts, tenderized

SAUCE

⅓ cup plain low-fat yogurt

½ teaspoon sea salt

1 garlic clove, minced

1-2 drops dōTERRA Lemon Essential Oil

1 tablespoon fresh parsley leaves, finely chopped

1. Place yogurt, Olive Oil, cumin, Lemon & Coriander Oils, and garlic in a small bowl. Place chicken breasts in a glass baking dish or in a re-sealable plastic bag. Spoon the yogurt mixture over the chicken and coat. Cover the dish or seal the bag and marinate in the refrigerator for a minimum of 5 hours.

2. Clean and brush grill grates with Olive Oil. Grill or broil chicken breasts 6 to 7 minutes each side, or until completely cooked through.

SAUCE

1. Blend all ingredients in a small bowl, and serve with Yogurt Chicken.

ROMAINE & SPINACH SALAD WITH
RASPBERRY VINAIGRETTE (page 79)

MINT COUSCOUS WITH ASPARAGUS
& SUNDRIED CRANBERRIES (page 74)

Side Dishes

DOUBLE COCONUT LIME RICE

(G) | (D) | (V)

The last time I made this for a cooking class, everyone just raved. The combination of Lime and Black Pepper Essential really hit the spot and had everyone coming back for 2nds, and 3rds.

PREPARATION: 10 minutes   **COOK TIME:** 20 minutes   **SERVES:** 6 to 8

2 cups basmati or long grain rice
3 tablespoons Extra Virgin Olive Oil, divided
1 teaspoon butter* (optional)
½ cup shredded coconut
2⅔ cups chicken broth**
1 (13-ounce) cans coconut milk
1 teaspoon sea salt
2-4 drops dōTERRA Lime Essential Oil
1 drop dōTERRA Black Pepper Oil (optional)
1 bunch scallions, thinly sliced

* Omit for vegan option
** Use vegetable broth for vegan option

1. Rinse rice until the water runs clear; drain.

2. Heat 2 tablespoons of Olive Oil and butter in a large skillet on medium-high. Add rice and coconut flakes; sauté for 3 to 5 minutes.

3. Stir in the chicken broth, coconut milk and salt. Cover and bring to a boil; reduce heat to low and cook for 20 minutes.

4. Remove it from the heat and keep it covered for a few minutes.

5. Combine remaining Olive, Lime and Pepper Oils; drizzle over warm rice and stir in green onions, until combined. Serve warm.

Featured on page 60 with Caribbean Shrimp With Warm Pineapple Salsa.

HUSKY MARJORAM & LIME GRILLED CORN

G

This grilled self-contained side dish will please even the pickiest of eaters. Infusing the flavorful essence of Marjoram, the zippy zest in Lime Essential Oil, and the perfect flavor of Parmesan cheese, they won't be picky for long. To be safe, I would make extra for those coming back for seconds.

PREPARATION: 35 minutes   **COOK TIME:** 25 minutes   **SERVES:** 6

6 large ears sweet corn, in husks
2 tablespoons Marjoram / EVOO Blend
2 garlic cloves, minced
½ teaspoon sea salt
2 drops dōTERRA Lime Essential Oil
¼ cup Extra Virgin Olive Oil, divided
½ cup grated Parmesan cheese
Sea salt and pepper

* See page 114

1. Soak corn in cold water for 30 minutes.

2. In a small bowl, combine Marjoram / EVOO Blend, garlic, ⅛ cup of Olive Oil, and ½ teaspoon salt; set aside.

3. Peel back the corn husks to 1 inch from the bottom and carefully remove the silk strands. Brush each ear of corn with Olive Oil Thyme mixture. Rewrap the corn in husks; tie to secure with kitchen string.

4. Place on a preheated grill, and cook for 25 minutes, turning occasionally.

5. In a small bowl, combine remaining Olive Oil and Lime Oil.

6. When the corn is cooked, remove the husks, brush with Lime Olive Oil mixture, and sprinkle with salt and pepper, to taste. Roll in Parmesan cheese and enjoy!!!

LEMON THYME GARLIC SNAP PEAS

Ⓖ Ⓓ Ⓥ

You will love the Olive Oil and citrus in this simple side dish. It's easy to make and even easier to eat. After only one bite, this mean, green vegetable will even have your kids asking you to make it for them again and again.

PREPARATION: 15 minutes   **COOK TIME:** 3 minutes   **SERVES:** 4 to 6

1 pound sugar snap peas, trimmed of stems and strings

2-3 garlic cloves, minced

2 tablespoons Extra Virgin Olive Oil, divided

1-2 drops dōTERRA Lemon Essential Oil

1 teaspoon Thyme / EVOO Blend

Sea salt and pepper to taste

* See page 114

1. In a large bowl, combine the snap peas, garlic, and 1 tablespoon of the Olive Oil.

2. In a small bowl, combine the Thyme / EVOO Blend and Lemon Oil; set aside.

3. Heat the remaining Olive Oil in a wok or other large skillet on medium-high, and stir fry for 3 to 5 minutes, or until lightly cooked and crisp.

4. Remove from heat and drizzle with the Lemon and EVOO mixture; add the salt and pepper, to taste. Toss to combine.

Featured on page 60 with Wild Orange & Grapefruit Soy Salmon and Potato Mashers With Lemon & Parsley.

MEDITERRANEAN CHICKPEA SALAD

G | D

My friend Leah once said, "If you're going to make this salad you might want to make a double batch." Intended to be a starter dish only, this salad can quickly turn into the main event. Watch out... this one disappears fast.

PREPARATION: 15 minutes   **SERVES:** 4

2   cups cooked or 1 (15-ounce) can garbanzo beans, drained

1   medium tomato, diced

½   medium red onion, chopped

2   medium garlic cloves, minced or pressed

2   tablespoons parsley, chopped

3-4   drops dōTERRA Lemon Essential Oil

¼   cup Extra Virgin Olive Oil

Sea salt and pepper

¼   cup Feta cheese (optional)

6   sliced Kalamata olives

1   teaspoon Rosemary / EVOO Blend*

* See page 114

1. Place the beans, tomato, onion, garlic, and parsley in a medium size bowl and toss together.

2. In a small bowl combine the Lemon Oil, Olive Oil, and salt and pepper, to taste. Serve it over a bed of fresh lettuce and save enough room for a second helping!

MINT COUSCOUS WITH ASPARAGUS & SUNDRIED CRANBERRIES

Ⓓ | Ⓥ

If you're searching for something simple, healthful, and different, look no further. Filled with the healthy goodness of green vegetables, tart cranberries, and a touch of Lemon and Peppermint Essential Oils, this delightful and filling Couscous might just have you skipping the rest of the meal.

PREPARATION: 12 minutes   **COOK TIME:** 10 minutes   **SERVES:** 6

2 cups boiling water

2 cups couscous

2 cups asparagus, cut 2-inch strips

6 tablespoons Extra Virgin Olive Oil

2 drops dōTERRA Lemon Essential Oil

1 drop dōTERRA Peppermint Essential Oil

1 drop dōTERRA Black Pepper Essential Oil (optional)

½ cup scallions, thinly sliced

¼ sun dried cranberries

1 handful baby spinach leaves

Sea salt and pepper

1. Pour 2 cups boiling water over the couscous; cover and let stand for 5 minutes.

2. In a large skillet, sauté asparagus in 2 tablespoons of the Olive Oil for 5 to 6 minutes. Season with salt and pepper; let cool to room temperature.

3. Blend remaining 4 tablespoons of Olive Oil, Lemon, Peppermint, and Black Pepper Oils in a small mixing bowl; set aside.

4. Place warm couscous in a large mixing bowl and fluff with a fork to separate clusters. Fold in asparagus, scallions, cranberries, and spinach. Pour Olive Oil over mixture and combine. Add salt and pepper, to taste.

Lemon

MINT COUSCOUS WITH ASPARAGUS
& SUNDRIED CRANBERRIES

POTATO MASHERS WITH LEMON & PARSLEY Ⓖ

Try a classy alternative and an old fashioned American favorite side. The Lemon and Pepper Essential Oils offer a little something zesty and zingy. So kick out the old and bring in the new, these Lemon Mashers are sure to be a hit at your next family gathering.

PREPARATION: 35 minutes   **COOK TIME:** 20 minutes   **SERVES:** 6 to 8

6   medium Yukon Gold potatoes, peeled and chopped

1   (8-ounce package) low-fat Neufchatel cream cheese

2   tablespoons Extra Virgin Olive Oil

1   cup milk

6   drops dōTERRA Lemon Essential Oil

1   drop dōTERRA Black Pepper Oil

2   tablespoons fresh parsley, finely chopped

Sea salt

1. Place the potatoes in a medium pot and boil for about 20 minutes, or until tender. Drain the potatoes and place in a large mixing bowl or stand mixer.

2. Add cream cheese and Olive Oil; blend on low speed. Slowly begin adding milk, Lemon and Pepper Oils. Increase speed to medium-high; mix until smooth.

3. Blend in parsley, and salt to taste. Serve warm with your favorite main dish.

Featured on page 60 with Wild Orange & Grapefruit Soy Salmon and Lemon Thyme Garlic Snap Peas.

ROASTED ZUCCHINI WITH RED PEPPERS & ONIONS Ⓖ Ⓓ Ⓥ

I love roasted vegetables and you will too thanks to the subtle flavor from the Basil infused Olive Oil, adding the perfect complement to these roasted veggies! It'll be the healthy "secret ingredient" your guests just can't figure out!

PREPARATION: 40 minutes   **COOK TIME:** 20 minutes   **SERVES:** 6 to 8

3 zucchini, cut lengthwise into ½-inch strips

3 cups red peppers, cut lengthwise into ½-inch strips

1 sweet yellow onion, thinly sliced

4-5 garlic cloves, minced

¼ cup Extra Virgin Olive Oil

Sea salt and pepper

1 drop dōTERRA Lemon Essential Oil

1 tablespoon Basil/EVOO Blend*

½ cup grated Parmesan cheese**

* See page 114

** Omit for Dairy Free and Vegan Options

1. Preheat oven to 450°F; lightly grease a 9x13-inch baking dish.

2. Combine the zucchini, peppers, onion, and garlic in prepared baking dish. Drizzle with Olive Oil and season with salt and pepper, to taste; mix well.

3. Roast in the oven until the vegetables are tender and slightly golden, about 20 minutes. Remove from the oven and combine Basil/EVOO Blend with Lemon Oil and drizzle over vegetables. Sprinkle with Parmesan cheese and serve warm.

ROMAINE & SPINACH SALAD W/ RASPBERRY VINAIGRETTE

ROMAINE & SPINACH SALAD W/RASPBERRY VINAIGRETTE

The crunch of candied almonds blended with the sweet and sour flavor in this undeniably healthful salad will leave you satisfied knowing you have eaten your greens and enjoyed them as well. With the sweetness of raspberries and a hint of Lime at the end, it won't be long before you will be craving this salad. **G | D | V**

PREPARATION: 15 minutes   **SERVES:** 6

½ cup Extra Virgin Olive Oil
¼ cup balsamic vinegar
1 tablespoon seedless raspberry preserves
⅓ cup cane sugar
2 drops dōTERRA Lime Essential Oil
2 teaspoons Dijon mustard
1 teaspoon Oregano/EVOO Blend*
½ teaspoon sea salt
¼ teaspoon ground black pepper

SALAD
1 large head Romaine lettuce, chopped
1 package baby spinach leaves
1 bunch green onions, chopped
⅓ cup sugared almonds (right)
1 pint fresh raspberries, for garnish

* See page 114

1. In a jar with a tight fitting lid, combine the Olive Oil, Lime Oil, Oregano/EVOO Blend, vinegar, salt, pepper, preserves, sugar and mustard. Shake until well blended; set aside while assembling salad.

2. Place prepared lettuce, spinach, and green onions in a large salad bowl; toss together.

3. Pour ¼ of the vinaigrette dressing into the salad and toss together, adding more dressing until desired taste. Refrigerate the remaining dressing to be used again for another delicious salad.

4. Gently fold in the sunflower seeds and raspberries; serve immediately.

SUGARED ALMONDS

1. Add 1 teaspoon Olive Oil and ⅓ cup almonds into a small skillet, turn the heat to high, toss in a couple of teaspoons of sugar, and cook until sugar is melted and almonds are brown; cool for 5 minutes. Be sure to watch it closely, it cooks quickly and burns easily.

SOUTHWESTERN PASTA SALAD

With the beautiful combination and zippy goodness found in Lemon and Coriander Essential Oils, this recipe delivers the wonderful flavor of the old Southwest. Bring it to your next potluck or picnic and watch it become the hit of the day!!!

PREPARATION: 10 minutes   **COOK TIME:** 35 minutes   **SERVES:** 6 to 8

8 cups cooked bowtie pasta

3 scallions, chopped

1 (15-ounce) can black beans, drained and rinsed

2 (4-ounce) cans mild green chilies, chopped

½ cup fresh Plum tomatoes, chopped

2 tablespoons Extra Virgin Olive Oil

1 (8-ounce) low-fat Neufchatel cream cheese

⅓ cup low-fat milk

¼ cup fresh lemon juice

4-6 drops dōTERRA Lemon Essential Oil

1-2 drops dōTERRA Coriander Essential Oil

1½ teaspoons cumin

1 teaspoon sea salt

1-2 garlic cloves, minced

¼ cup grated Parmesan cheese

1. In a large mixing bowl, add the pasta, scallions, beans, chilies, tomatoes, and Olive Oil; toss the mixture until well blended.

2. Place the cream cheese in a medium mixing bowl. Cover and heat in the microwave for about 1 minute or until very hot. Add the milk and stir until combined. Add lemon juice, Lemon and Coriander Oils, cumin, salt, garlic, and Parmesan; Stir until well blended.

3. Pour mixture over pasta and blend all ingredients together. Serve as a side dish, appetizer, or salad.

SUMMER CORN SALAD WITH CORIANDER & LIME

I just love fresh corn in the summer, who doesn't? But when you make your family and friends this delicious potpourri of vegetables, infused with the healing benefits found in Essential Oils, their love for corn will be taken to a whole new level.

PREPARATION: 10 minutes   **SERVES:** 6 to 8

1 (16-ounce) package frozen corn, thawed
2 small zucchinis, diced
½ large red pepper, diced
1 large garlic clove, crushed
½ small onion, chopped
1 (4-ounce) can diced green chilies, drained
¼ cup Extra Virgin Olive Oil
2-3 drops dōTERRA Lime Essential Oil
1 drop dōTERRA Coriander Essential Oil
½ tablespoon red wine vinegar
¾ teaspoon ground cumin
1 teaspoon sea salt
¼ teaspoon pepper
1 avocado, diced

1. Place corn, zucchini, red pepper, garlic, onion, and chilies in a large bowl; toss to blend.

2. In a small bowl, mix together the Olive Oil, Lime and Coriander Oils, vinegar, cumin, salt and pepper. Pour over salad and refrigerate a minimum of 1 hour.

3. Gently fold in avocado just prior to serving.

LEMON INFUSED CREAM OF
BROCCOLI SOUP (page 91)

ROASTED TOMATO BASIL
& FENNEL SOUP (page 92)

Soups

CORN CHOWDER & THYME

A yummy soup with the essence of thyme and the sweet aftertaste only fresh corn can deliver. Make it in the summer when the corn is fresh and plentiful, or just make it any old thyme.

PREPARATION: 15 minutes   **COOK TIME:** 25 minutes   **SERVES:** Serves: 6 to 8

2 tablespoons Extra Virgin Olive Oil
1 onion, diced
½ cup red bell pepper, diced
2 garlic cloves, minced
4 tablespoons all-purpose flour
6 cups chicken broth
2 medium size potatoes, peeled and diced
1 (15-ounce) can evaporated milk
1 cup heavy cream
5 cups fresh or frozen corn
1 drop dōTERRA Thyme Essential Oil
¾ teaspoon sea salt
½ teaspoon white pepper
¼ cup fresh parsley, chopped

1. In a soup pot heat Olive Oil on medium. Add onion, red pepper, and garlic; sauté until soft, about 8 to 10 minutes.

2. Sprinkle the flour over onion and garlic mixture; stir until well coated. Add broth and potatoes. Boil for 5 to 7 minutes, or until the potatoes begin to soften. Stir in milk, cream, salt, and pepper.

3. Add corn and simmer about 10 minutes. Add Thyme Oil and simmer another 2 minutes.

4. Stir in parsley and ladle the soup into bowls. Swirl Olive Oil into each bowl and serve.

CREAMY TOMATO & MINT SOUP

An unlikely but surprisingly warming and delicious soup, this Mint laced oldie but goodie will have you feeling warm and satisfied in no time. Enjoy it with a piece of your favorite bread or crackers, either way you look at it, this tasty surprise will be a refreshing addition to your family meals.

PREPARATION: 10 minutes   **COOK TIME:** 45 to 50 minutes   **SERVES:** 6 to 8

3 tablespoons Extra Virgin Olive Oil

1 medium onion, finely chopped

1 tablespoon garlic, minced

1 tablespoon all-purpose flour

4 cups tomatoes, chopped

8 cups chicken broth

2 tablespoons tomato paste

Sea salt

2 cups heavy (or whipping) cream

2 drops dōTERRA Peppermint Essential Oil

1 drop dōTERRA Black Pepper Essential Oil (optional)

Additional Olive Oil, for garnish

1. Heat Olive Oil in a large pot, and sauté onions and garlic on medium for about 10 minutes, or until onions are translucent but not browned. Add flour and cook for 3 minutes, making a paste.

2. Add tomatoes, broth, tomato paste, and salt; stir. Bring it to a boil; then reduce the heat and simmer uncovered for 30 minutes. Stir occasionally, or until the tomatoes become very soft.

3. Puree in small batches in the blender, and return soup to the pot. Turn heat to low and gently blend in cream and simmer for 5 minutes, stirring occasionally. Remove from heat and stir in Peppermint and Black Pepper Oils. Ladle soup into bowls and drizzle it with Olive Oil. Serve with warm garlic bread.

HEALING SOUP WITH CILANTRO & GINGER Ⓖ|Ⓓ

This delicious and healing soup works fantastically on sore throats and seasonal colds. But don't wait until you are not feeling well as it is so delicious and warming anytime you are in the mood for something comforting and fragrant.

PREPARATION: 20 minutes   **COOK TIME:** 20 minutes   **SERVES:** 6

1½-2 pounds chicken breast, sliced thinly
½ teaspoon sea salt
½ teaspoon ground white pepper
1 tablespoon cornstarch
3 cups chicken broth
3 cups water
1 small bunch cilantro leaves, chopped
½ teaspoon Extra Virgin Olive Oil
½ teaspoon sesame oil (optional)
2-3 drops dōTERRA Ginger Essential Oil
1 drop dōTERRA Coriander Essential Oil
2 boiled eggs, peeled and sliced
Cilantro leaves, for garnish

1. Rinse and partially freeze chicken for 2 to 4 hours. Remove from freezer and slice thinly.

2. Sprinkle salt and pepper on chicken slices and coat with cornstarch; let rest for 15 minutes.

3. In a large pot, bring broth and water to a boil. Turn heat to low and add cilantro; continue to simmer for 10 minutes.

4. Using a small bowl, combine Olive Oil, sesame oil, Ginger and Coriander Oils; set aside.

5. While simmering, stir in prepared chicken and cook for another 3 to 5 minutes. Remove from heat and stir in blended Oils. Garnish with cilantro leaves and sliced eggs. Serve hot.

Coriander
Ginger
Zingiber officinale
15 ml
Essential Oil Supplement
Coriander
Coriandrum sativum
15 ml

LEEK & POTATO SOUP WITH LEMON & THYME Ⓖ

Leeks are luscious and if you haven't ever used them in a soup, you must try this soup at least once. You will never go back to onions in a creamy soup again! They add a delicate touch to this Thyme tested Potato Soup. Try sprinkling a little fresh crushed basil on the soup for garnish, and you have a winner.

PREPARATION: 15 minutes   **COOK TIME:** 25 minutes   **SERVES:** 6 to 8

¼ cup Extra Virgin Olive Oil
1½ cups leeks (white part only), thinly sliced
½ cup celery, chopped
5 cups chicken broth
4 large potatoes, peeled and chopped
2 cups milk
2 cups half and half
Sea salt and pepper
3 drops dōTERRA Lemon Essential Oil
1 tablespoon dōTERRA Thyme/EVOO Blend*
¼ cup grated Parmesan cheese

* See page 114

1. In a large soup pot on low heat, add the Olive Oil, leeks, and celery; sauté for 5 to 8 minutes, or until the mixture appears soft.

2. Increase heat to high, add broth and potatoes; boil until potatoes until they to fall apart (about 10 minutes). Remove from heat; transfer mixture into a blender and puree in batches until smooth.

3. Return soup to pot, stir in milk, half and half, and salt and pepper to taste and heat for 5 minutes, or until warm and bubbly. Remove and stir in Lemon Oil and Thyme/EVOO Blend.

4. Ladle the hot soup into bowls and sprinkle it with Parmesan cheese.

THAI LEMONGRASS SOUP WITH GARLIC & SHRIMP Ⓖ Ⓓ

When you are craving a strong, powerful, health boosting soup, look no further. This Thai favorite offers the perfect marriage of spice, sweet, salty, and sour with the healing power of Lemongrass, Lime, Coriander, and Ginger Essential Oils. Its robust, aromatic essence will clear your sinuses and having you feeling better in no time. Just the thought of its deep and delicious flavor will have you making it for no particular reason at all.

PREPARATION: 15 minutes   **COOK TIME:** 15 minutes   **SERVES:** 4

6 cups chicken broth

3-4 garlic cloves, minced

¾ teaspoon chili pepper flakes

1½ shiitake mushrooms, sliced

1 lime; juiced

2 tablespoons fish sauce

1 tablespoon soy sauce

1½ cups coconut milk

12 medium to large shrimp, shells removed

2 tablespoons Basil/EVOO Blend (see page 114)

1 drop dōTERRA Lime Essential Oil

2 drops dōTERRA Lemongrass Essential Oil

2 drops dōTERRA Ginger Essential Oil

1 drop each dōTERRA Coriander Essential Oil

Sea salt and pepper

Hot chili oil (optional)

Cilantro leaves, for garnish

1. Heat the broth in a large pot on high and bring to a light boil.

2. Reduce heat to medium and add garlic, pepper flakes, mushrooms, lime juice, fish sauce and soy sauce; simmer 3 to 5 minutes.

3. Add coconut milk and shrimp; simmer for about 3 minutes or until shrimp turns pink.

4. Remove from heat and stir in Basil/EVOO Blend, Lime, Lemongrass, Ginger, and Coriander Oils. Add salt and pepper, to taste, and simmer for 1 to 2 minutes. Ladle soup into bowls and add a little hot chili oil if you dare. Top with a generous sprinkling of fresh cilantro and ENJOY!

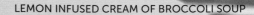

LEMON INFUSED CREAM OF BROCCOLI SOUP

A pleasant tasting soup laced with the uplifting flavor of Lemon Essential Oil, will delight those who enjoy the taste of zesty tartness.

PREPARATION: 20 minutes   **COOK TIME:** 15 minutes   **SERVES:** 6 to 8

¼ cup Extra Virgin Olive Oil
½ cup onion, finely chopped
2 large stalks celery, finely chopped
6 tablespoons all-purpose flour
3 cups chicken broth
3 cups milk
½ teaspoon sea salt
¼ teaspoon pepper
4 cups fresh broccoli, chopped
1 garlic clove, crushed
6-8 drops dōTERRA Lemon Essential Oil
Mild Cheddar Cheese (optional)

1. Using a medium sized pot, add Olive Oil, onion, and celery. Sauté on medium-high for 5 minutes, or until onions become translucent.

2. Reduce heat to low; blend in flour until vegetable mixture resembles a paste.*

3. Increase heat to high and add the broth and milk; stir continually until the paste mixture is completely dissolved. Continue cooking on high for 3 to 5 minutes or until sauce is thickened.

4. Reduce heat again to low and stir in the broccoli, garlic, and Lemon Oil. Top with cheese and serve hot with garlic toast.

* This paste is also known as a roux; the mixture of fat and flour that is used for thickening sauces and soups. If it is dissolved completely as described, you will not have clumps in your soup!

ROASTED TOMATO BASIL & FENNEL SOUP Ⓖ|Ⓓ

The distinct flavors of Basil, Fennel, and Oregano Essential Oils in this roasted soup, offers just the right amount of taste for an afternoon snack. Or you could pair it with a grilled provolone cheese sandwich and call it a meal.

PREPARATION: 20 minutes   **COOK TIME:** 2½ hours   **SERVES:** 4 to 6

2½ pounds fresh tomatoes
Sea salt and pepper, for roasting
1 sweet onion, chopped
4 garlic cloves, minced
5 cups chicken broth
1 teaspoon sea salt
½ teaspoon pepper
1 tablespoon Basil/EVOO Blend*
2 teaspoons Fennel/EVOO Blend*
½ teaspoon Oregano/EVOO Blend*
⅓ cup Extra Virgin Olive Oil, divided
2 tablespoons balsamic vinegar

* See page 114

1. Preheat oven to 350°F and line a rimmed baking sheet with foil.

2. Core the tomatoes and cut them in half. Arrange the cut sides up on prepared baking sheet and brush tomatoes with Olive Oil; lightly sprinkle with salt and pepper. Bake until tomatoes are shriveled and soft, and bottoms are browned, about 2 hours.

3. In a soup pot, add onion, garlic, and 2 tablespoons of Olive Oil. Sauté 5 to 7 minutes or until the onion is slightly softened. Add the broth, tomatoes, salt, and pepper; stir. Bring to a boil and reduce heat to simmer for 15 minutes.

4. Transfer the tomato mixture into a blender or food processor and process until smooth; return to pot. Stir in EVOO Blends, and simmer for another 2 minutes.

5. In a small mixing bowl, whisk together remaining Olive Oil and vinegar. Ladle soup into bowls. Garnish with a drizzle of vinegar mixture. Serve with green salad and garlic bread.

Fennel

ROASTED TOMATO BASIL & FENNEL SOUP

LAVENDER & VANILLA CUPCAKES WITH
TANGERINE CREAM CHEESE FROSTING (page 101)

PEPPERMINT MAGIC HARD SHELL
ICE CREAM DRIZZLE (page 111)

Desserts

LEMON YOGURT CAKE WITH BLUEBERRY & HONEY PUREE

Okay lemon lovers, you've met your match. Packed with the powerful taste of Lemon Essential Oil and blueberry bliss, this cake is sure to wow your family and friend.

PREPARATION: 25 minutes   **COOK TIME:** 50 to 60 minutes   **SERVES:** 10 to 12

½ cup Extra Virgin Olive Oil*
1 cup plain low-fat yogurt
1 cup cane sugar
3 large eggs
5 drops dōTERRA Lemon Essential Oil
1 teaspoon lemon zest
⅓ cup lemon juice, freshly squeezed
2 teaspoons pure vanilla extract
1½ cups all-purpose flour
2 teaspoons baking powder
½ teaspoon sea salt

BLUEBERRY & HONEY PUREE

1 cup fresh or frozen blueberries
¼ cup honey
1-2 drops dōTERRA Lemon Essential Oil
Pinch of sea salt
Raspberries, blueberries, and mint sprigs, for garnish

* Use Mild Flavor Extra Virgin Olive Oil or Pure Olive Oil

1. Preheat the oven to 350°F and coat a loaf pan generously with cooking spray.

2. In a mixing bowl, add Olive Oil, yogurt, sugar, eggs, Lemon Oil, lemon zest, lemon juice, and vanilla; mix on medium speed until blended.

3. Slowly add flour, baking powder, and salt into the blended ingredients and mix together until combined and smooth. Pour the batter into the prepared loaf pan and bake for about 50 minutes, or until a toothpick placed in the center of the loaf comes out clean.

4. Using a food processor, chop the blueberries. Add honey, Lemon Oil, & a pinch of salt; blend until smooth. Put in a bowl and set aside.

5. When your cake is finished baking, remove from oven, and cool for 10 minutes. Remove cake from pan and place on a flat dessert dish. Pour blueberry mixture over the top, garnish and serve immediately!!!

GINGER SNAP & LEMON CREAM COOKIEWICHES

Try something deliciously different, yet beautifully satisfying. These Cookiewiches offer up a delightful aroma of spicy goodness that is not soon to be forgotten. With the enchanting combination of Ginger, Cassia, and Lemon Essential Oils, and the healthy goodness in Olive Oil, this is one cookie you can feel good about sinking your teeth into.

PREPARATION: 30 minutes   **COOK TIME:** 10 minutes   **SERVES:** 16 Cookiewiches

COOKIES

- ½ cup Extra Virgin Olive Oil*
- 1 cup brown sugar
- 1 egg
- ¼ cup dark molasses
- 1 teaspoon fresh ginger, finely minced
- 1 teaspoon pure vanilla extract
- 1 drop dōTERRA Ginger Essential Oil
- 1 drop dōTERRA Cassia Essential Oil
- 2¼ cups all-purpose flour
- 1 teaspoon ground cinnamon
- 1¼ teaspoons baking soda
- ½ teaspoon sea salt
- ⅓ cup cane sugar, for cookie rolling

* Use Mild Flavor Extra Virgin Olive Oil or Pure Olive Oil

LEMON CREAM

- 4 ounces low-fat Neufchatel cream cheese, softened
- ½ stick of butter, softened
- 2 teaspoons pure vanilla extract
- 6-8 drops dōTERRA Lemon Essential Oil
- Pinch of sea salt
- 3-4 cups of powdered sugar
- 1-2 tablespoons of milk

Featured on page 99.

GINGER SNAP & LEMON CREAM COOKIEWICHES (CONT.)

COOKIES

1. Preheat oven to 350°F and spray baking sheets with Olive Oil cooking spray.

2. In mixing bowl, add the Olive Oil, brown sugar, and egg; mix on medium speed until well blended. Add molasses, ginger, vanilla, Ginger and Cassia Oils, and mix until combined.

3. Add flour, cinnamon, soda, and salt; mix until well blended. Cover and allow to rest in the refrigerator for 15 to 30 minutes.

4. Roll dough into 2-inch balls, roll in sugar, and place 2 inches apart on prepared baking sheets. Using the bottom of a glass, gently press down on cookie ball to flatten slightly.

5. Bake 8 to 10 minutes. Cool cookies on a wire rack.

LEMON CREAM

6. In a mixing bowl, add cream cheese, butter, vanilla, Lemon Oil, and salt. Blend together until well mixed.

7. While turning mixer to a low speed, slowly begin adding powdered sugar 1 cup at a time. Once all of the powdered sugar has been blended, continue to mix until frosting is fluffy and beautiful

8. Spread frosting on the bottom side of a cookie, and place another cookie on top.

9. And that is how you make a cookiewich.

West African women in Senegal have been known to weave belts of ginger to bring back their partners reproductive potency.

Aroma & Olive Oil The Essentials of Healthy & Delicious Cuisine

GINGER SNAP & LEMON CREAM COOKIEWICHES

LAVENDER & VANILLA CUPCAKES WITH
TANGERINE CREAM CHEESE FROSTING

LAVENDER & VANILLA CUPCAKES WITH TANGERINE CREAM CHEESE FROSTING

A hint of floral essence perfectly enhances this sweet and delightful dessert. The calming aroma found in the Lavender Essential Oil combined with the citrus goodness of the Tangerine Essential Oil will deliver the perfect ending to any meal. Enjoy!!!

PREPARATION: 25 minutes   **COOK TIME:** 20 minutes   **SERVES:** 18

CUPCAKES

- 1½ cups cane sugar
- 1½ vanilla beans, scraped (optional)
- 2⅓ cups plus 2 tablespoons, cake flour, not self-rising
- 2¼ teaspoons baking powder
- ¾ teaspoon baking soda
- ¾ teaspoon sea salt
- ¾ cup Extra Virgin Olive Oil*
- 3 large eggs, room temperature
- ½ cup Greek yogurt
- 2 tablespoons pure vanilla extract (use 3 tablespoons if not using vanilla beans)
- ⅔ cup whole milk
- 3 drops dōTERRA Lavender Essential Oil

FROSTING

- 4 ounces low-fat Neufchatel cream cheese, softened
- 2 ounces butter
- 2 teaspoons pure vanilla extract
- 4-6 drops dōTERRA Tangerine Essential Oil**
- 4-5 cups powdered sugar

Orange slices, for garnish

Lavender sprigs, for garnish

* Use Mild Flavor Extra Virgin Olive Oil or Pure Olive Oil

** Substitute Wild Orange Essential Oil if Tangerine Oil is unavailable

LAVENDER & VANILLA CUPCAKES WITH TANGERINE CREAM CHEESE FROSTING (CONT.)

1. Preheat oven to 350°F and line 18 to 25 muffin tins with cupcake liners.

2. In a small mixing bowl, combine sugar and vanilla bean seeds; blend using the back of a tablespoon to loosen any clumps of seeds, and set aside.

3. In a large mixing bowl, sift together cake flour, baking powder, baking soda, and salt; set aside.

4. In mixing bowl, add Olive Oil, eggs, yogurt, vanilla, milk, and Lavender Oil; mix for 1 minute. Add vanilla bean sugar mixture and mix until well blended. Add flour mixture and blend until completely combined.

5. Fill cupcake liners ⅔ full, and bake for 12 to 15 minutes, or until a toothpick inserted into the center comes out clean. Remove from oven and cool completely before frosting.

FROSTING

1. In a large mixing bowl, beat cream cheese, butter, vanilla, and Tangerine Oil together until it is smooth and creamy. Add sugar, 1 cup at a time on low speed until completely combined. Increase the speed to high and mix until very fluffy and smooth. Frost cooled cupcakes and try not to eat the whole batch before serving them!

There are some things, after all, that Sally Owens knows for certain: Always throw spilled salt over your left shoulder. Keep rosemary by your garden gate. Add pepper to your mashed potatoes. Plant roses and lavender, for luck. Fall in love whenever you can.

WILD ORANGE & CHOCOLATE HABANERO COOKIES

This surprisingly yummy cookie made with heart healthy Olive Oil has a hint of Orange and a spicy kick that will awaken your taste buds and rock your world!!! For sweet & tasty cookies without the kick, just omit the Habanero pepper and savor.

PREPARATION: 15 minutes   **COOK TIME:** 10 minutes   **SERVES:** 12 to 16

½ cup Extra Virgin Olive Oil*

1½ cups cane sugar

3 large eggs, beaten

3 tablespoons water or milk

2 drops dōTERRA Wild Orange Essential Oil

½ to 1 Habanero pepper, chopped (if you dare**)

2 teaspoons pure vanilla extract

½ cup unsweetened dark cocoa

2⅔ cups all-purpose flour

2 teaspoons baking powder

¾ teaspoon sea salt

1¼ cups mini chocolate chips

¾ cup cane sugar, for rolling

* Use Mild Flavor Extra Virgin Olive Oil or Pure Olive Oil.

1. Preheat oven to 375°F and lightly coat large baking sheets with Olive Oil cooking spray.

2. In mixing bowl add the Olive Oil, sugar, eggs, and milk; blend until completely mixed.

3. Add the vanilla, Orange Oil, Habanero pepper, and cocoa; mix until blended.

4. Add flour, baking powder, and salt; blend well. Mix in chocolate chips, until combined.

5. Drop by teaspoonfuls or a small size cookie scoop into sugar and roll until coated.

6. Place 3 drops per row (these cookies spread). Press with the bottom of a glass; bake for 8 to 10 minutes. Remove from oven and let cool. These cookies may seem cool to the touch, but believe me, they are hot!

*** THIS COOKIE COMES WITH A WARNING! ** Habanero peppers are very hot!!! Wear food preparation gloves and do not touch your eyes or your face after chopping. Please warn of spiciness to those you share these cookies with.*

ORANGE & CHOCOLATE BUNDT W/BASIL CHOCOLATE GLAZE

This blend of wild orange, chocolate, and basil chocolate is a pleasant surprise. Discover a new world of flavor!

PREPARATION: 10 minutes   **COOK TIME:** 45 minutes   **SERVES:** 8 to 10

1 package devil's food cake mix
1 small package instant chocolate pudding mix
1 cup low-fat vanilla yogurt
⅔ cup Extra Virgin Olive Oil*
4 eggs, beaten
4 drops dōTERRA Wild Orange Essential Oil
½ cup warm water
1 cup semi-sweet chocolate chips

GLAZE

1 cup semi-sweet chocolate chips
¼ cup Extra Virgin Olive Oil*
1 tablespoon honey
Pinch of sea salt
1 teaspoon pure vanilla extract
1 tablespoon Basil/EVOO Blend**

* Use Mild Flavor Extra Virgin Olive Oil or Pure Olive Oil
** See page 114

1. Preheat the oven to 350°F and coat a Bundt pan generously with olive oil cooking spray.

2. In a large bowl, add cake mix, pudding mix, yogurt, Olive Oil, eggs, Orange Oil, & water. Blend on medium speed until completely mixed. Add chocolate chips and blend until completely combined; pour batter into prepared Bundt pan.

3. Bake for 45-50 minutes, or until toothpick inserted comes out clean. Cool cake thoroughly for 5 minutes and invert on to a serving plate; glaze immediately.

GLAZE

1. Approximately 5 to 10 minutes before the cake is finished baking, prepare glaze.

2. In a small glass bowl, add chocolate chips, Olive Oil, and honey. Place in microwave on high for 30 seconds at a time, or until chocolate is almost melted; stir and repeat the process until the chocolate is completely melted.

3. Add salt, vanilla, and EVOO Blend; mix until well combined. Drizzle over cake while it's still warm.

ORANGE & CHOCOLATE BUNDT
WITH BASIL CHOCOLATE GLAZE

PUMPKIN CUPCAKES WITH CINNAMON CREAM CHEESE GLAZE

PUMPKIN CUPCAKES W/CINNAMON CREAM CHEESE GLAZE

Everyone needs some spice in their lives every now and then, and these cupcakes surely fit the bill for sweet and spicy like no other. With the added benefits found in Cinnamon and Ginger Oils, your heart and tummy will sing.

PREPARATION: 25 minutes   **COOK TIME:** 30 minutes   **SERVES:** 24 cupcakes

1 cup Extra Virgin Olive Oil*
2 eggs, beaten
1¼ cups cane sugar
1 cup packed brown sugar
1 (15-ounce) can pumpkin puree
2 drops dōTERRA Cinnamon Essential Oil
2 drops dōTERRA Ginger Essential Oil
3 cups all-purpose flour
1 teaspoon each ground nutmeg
2 teaspoons baking soda
1 teaspoon sea salt

GLAZE

4 ounces Neufchatel cream cheese, softened
1 cup powdered sugar
¼ cup (½ stick) butter, softened
½ teaspoon pure vanilla extract
1 drop dōTERRA Cinnamon Essential Oil

* Use Mild Flavor Extra Virgin Olive Oil or Pure Olive Oil

1. Preheat oven to 350°F and place 24 cupcake liners in muffin tins.

2. In a large mixer bowl, cream together Olive Oil, eggs, and white & brown sugars. Add pumpkin puree, Cinnamon and Ginger Oils, and mix until well blended; set aside.

3. In medium size bowl, sift together flour, nutmeg, soda, and salt. Fold into pumpkin mixture and blend until well completely combined. Do not over mix.

4. Spoon batter into muffin tins and bake for 25 to 35 minutes, or until a toothpick inserted into the center of the cupcake comes out clean. Glaze while hot; cool and remove from tins.

GLAZE

1. In a medium bowl, add all glaze ingredients and mix until smooth. Using a teaspoon, glaze each cupcake individually. Cool at room temperature and serve.

TANGERINE DREAMSICLE KRISPY RICE TREATS Ⓖ|Ⓓ

Originally created in the 1920's for a Girl Scout campfire; this treat has come full circle. With the well-known calming properties found in Tangerine Essential Oil, this treat is the perfect finish after a stress filled day.

PREPARATION: 10 minutes   **COOK TIME:** 10 minutes   **SERVES:** 12

¼ cup Extra Virgin Olive Oil*
4 cups miniature marshmallows
Pinch of sea salt
1 teaspoon pure vanilla extract
⅓ cup white chocolate chips
6-8 drops dōTERRA Tangerine Essential Oil**
6 cups Krispy Rice Cereal®

* Use Mild Flavor Extra Virgin Olive Oil or Pure Olive Oil

** Substitute Wild Orange Essential Oil if Tangerine Oil
is unavailable

1. In a large pot, heat Olive Oil on medium. Add marshmallows and salt; stir until completely melted.

2. Remove from heat and blend in the vanilla, white chocolate chips and Tangerine Oil.

3. Add cereal & stir until well combined; pour mixture into a 13x9-inch baking dish sprayed with Olive Oil cooking spray. Spread and press down with a sprayed spatula; cool completely.

Olive oil is technically a fruit juice rather than an oil. The olives are pressed to release their juices just like an orange or a lemon is pressed to release their essential oil.

TANGERINE
DREAMSICLE
KRISPY RICE
TREATS

PEPPERMINT MAGIC HARD SHELL
ICE CREAM DRIZZLE

Ⓓ

Intrigue adults and children alike with this chocolate ice-cream coating. Add in a couple of drops of Tangerine Essential Oil and you will really have your guests intrigued and asking, "How did you do it?" To which you can modestly reply, "Simple... it's pure Magic!"

PREPARATION: 10 minutes   **COOK TIME:** 6 minutes   **SERVES:** 10 to 12

12 ounces semi-sweet chocolate chips*
4 tablespoons Extra Virgin Olive Oil**
2 drops dōTERRA Peppermint
   Essential Oil

* Use Gluten Free chocolate chips
** Use Mild Flavor Extra Virgin Olive Oil
   or Pure Olive Oil

1. Place chocolate and Olive Oil in a glass bowl and microwave on high for 30 seconds at a time, or until chocolate is almost melted; stir and repeat the process until chocolate is completely melted. Stir in Peppermint Oil and drizzle over ice cream or frozen yogurt.

2. Store it in an airtight glass container at room temperature. Do not place in refrigerator. When ready to use, heat in the microwave for 30 seconds before use.

MINTY VANILLA & WILD ORANGE TRUFFLES

Go wild for the taste and antioxidant power found in Wild Orange Essential Oil. These truffles are so tasty and so filling, it does not take much to satisfy the orange lover inside you.

PREPARATION: 20 minutes plus chilling time   **SERVES:** 10

¾ cup heavy cream
1 teaspoon pure vanilla extract
1 drop dōTERRA Lemon Essential Oil
4-6 drops dōTERRA Wild Orange Essential Oil
12 ounces white chocolate chips

COATING

1 lb chopped white chocolate, for tempering
1 tablespoon Extra Virgin Olive Oil*
1-2 drops dōTERRA Peppermint Essential Oil
   (optional)

* Use Mild Flavor Extra Virgin Olive Oil or Pure Olive Oil

1. Prepare a baking sheet by lining it with parchment paper; lightly spray with Olive Oil cooking spray.

2. Pour cream into a medium saucepan and simmer on low, until bubbles begin to appear. Remove from heat, stir in vanilla, Lemon and Wild Orange Oils, cover, and allow the flavor to infuse for 30 minutes.

3. Place white chocolate in a medium size bowl and melt in the microwave for 1 minute.

4. Return cream to heat to allow it to warm (not boil).

5. Once reheated, slowly pour melted chocolate over vanilla orange mixture, and blend until combined.

6. Cover & cool at room temperature for 30 minutes. Place in the refrigerator at least 4 hours or overnight. When mixture is firm, place on prepared baking sheet.

COATING

1. Place chocolate and Olive Oil in a glass bowl and microwave on high for 30 seconds at a time, or until chocolate is almost melted; stir and repeat until completely melted. Stir in Peppermint oil.

2. Using 2 forks, dip one truffle at a time, and return them to the baking sheet. Once all truffles are dipped, refrigerate for a minimum of 1 hour. Remove & enjoy!

PEPPERMINT & CHOCOLATE LOVE TRUFFLES (G)

It has been said... "If you love someone set them free." But I say if you love someone, make them these peppermint truffles and they will come back, love you more, and not be able to stay away. Who knew that a tiny piece of chocolate could do so much for love?

PREPARATION: 2½ hours   **COOK TIME:** 2 minutes   **SERVES:** 24 to 28 truffles

⅓ cup semi-sweet or milk chocolate chips
1 teaspoon Extra Virgin Olive Oil*
4 ounces Neufchatel cream cheese
4 cups powdered sugar

COATING

⅓ cup semi-sweet chocolate chips
1 tablespoon Extra Virgin Olive Oil*
2 drops dōTERRA Peppermint Essential Oil

* Use Mild Flavor Extra Virgin Olive Oil or Pure Olive Oil
** If you are anti-microwave a double boiler will also work

1. Place ⅓ cup chocolate and the Olive Oil in a medium size glass bowl and microwave** on high for 30 seconds at a time, or until chocolate is almost melted; stir and repeat the process until the chocolate is completely melted. Allow the chocolate mixture to cool for 5 minutes.

2. In a mixer, add softened cream cheese, and blend on medium speed until smooth. Add powdered sugar and mix until well blended; scoop, and shape into small 1½-inch balls. Place on greased baking sheet and refrigerate for 1 hour.

COATING

1. In another small glass bowl, add chocolate chips and Olive Oil. Heat in microwave for 1 minute or until chocolate chips are completely melted.

2. Blend in Peppermint Oil; coat cooled truffles and place back in the refrigerator to solidify.

3. Remove chocolate balls from refrigerator, dip in the chocolate mixture, and return to baking sheet.

4. After dipping truffles, place back in the refrigerator for about 15 to 30 minutes. Serve to family & friends!

ESSENTIAL OIL & EVOO BLENDS RECIPES

Combining Extra Virgin Olive Oil and Essential Oils delivers both the heart healthy benefits found in EVOO and the healing properties found in the Essential Oils. I hope you will enjoy my Essential Oil/EVOO Blends.

For each blend, you will need:

> 1 (4-6 ounce) blue or amber glass bottle with sealing cap
> 4 ounces Extra Virgin Olive Oil

Once ingredients are combined, seal, shake, and cook.

BASIL/EVOO BLEND
4 drops Basil Essential Oil

ROSEMARY/EVOO BLEND
3 drops Rosemary Essential Oil

THYME/EVOO BLEND
3 drops Thyme Essential Oil

OREGANO/EVOO BLEND
2 drops Oregano Essential Oil

FENNEL/EVOO BLEND
3 drops Fennel Essential Oil

MARJORAM/EVOO BLEND
4 drops Marjoram Essential Oil

CONVERTING TO OLIVE OIL

BUTTER, MARGARINE, or SHORTENING	OLIVE OIL
1 teaspoon	¾ teaspoon
1 tablespoon	2 teaspoons
2 tablespoons	1⅓ tablespoons
¼ cup	3 tablespoons
⅓ cup	¼ cup
½ cup	¼ cup + 1 tablespoon
⅔ cup	⅓-½ cup
¾ cup	½ cup + 1 tablespoon
1 cup	⅔-¾ cup

This chart shows approximate conversions. When converting your favorite dessert recipe into a healthier version you may need to use a little more or a little less heart-healthy Olive Oil. Enjoy experimenting!

*Olive oil has 5mg of flavenoid polyphenols for every 10 grams of oil.
These polyphenols are natural anti—oxidants that can prevent heart disease,
lower cholesterol and blood pressure, and reduce the overall effects of aging.*

GLUTEN-FREE OPTIONS

The challenge of baking gluten-free with recipes requiring flour can be daunting. The gluten-free flour recipes below can help you. These blends are not exact replacements for wheat flour with traditional baked goods, but they can get you close to the results you want. Try experimenting with these blends in your own recipes.

GLUTEN-FREE FLOUR BLEND #1

1 cup sorghum flour (or brown rice flour, if avoiding sorghum)

1 cup tapioca starch, corn starch, or potato starch (not potato flour!)

½ cup almond flour, G-F millet, G-F buckwheat flour, G-F coconut flour, or garbanzo flour

1 teaspoon xanthan gum or guar

Mix all of the ingredients together and store in an airtight container in the refrigerator.

GLUTEN-FREE FLOUR BLEND #2

1 cup sorghum flour

¾ cup potato, tapioca, or corn starch

½ cup garbanzo flour

½ cup buckwheat flour or cornmeal

¼ cup almond or coconut flour

1½ teaspoons xanthan gum

Mix all of the ingredients together and store in an airtight container in the refrigerator.

GLUTEN-FREE FOR THICKENING

There are a few recipes containing wheat flour used to make a roux (the mixture of fat and flour that is used for thickening sauces and soups). For those recipes, I have a few alternatives which are gluten-free. The measurements are the same, but rather than making a roux by adding the wheat flour (during the sauté process), just sauté as directed in the recipe and after all liquids are added to the soup, blend in the starch mixture of your choice and boil until thickened.

For every 1 tablespoon of starch, mix with 1 tablespoon of water before adding to soup recipes.

• Arrowroot starch

• Cornstarch

• Rice Flour

• Tapioca starch

• Sorghum Flour

DAIRY ALTERNATIVES

For people who have an intolerance or allergy to lactose based products, dairy is not an option. However, now you can enjoy all of the recipes in this cookbook because I have some fantastic alternatives which will allow the delicious taste of my recipes to shine without dairy.

TIP: When shopping for lactose-free products, always read labels. Some products which are labeled "milk-free" or "lactose-free" may actually contain small amounts of lactose.

Listed below is a quick guide to lactose-free cooking.

EVAPORATED MILK SUBSTITUTIONS

Using lactose-free, soy, or coconut milk:

Use double the amount needed of lactose-free milk, place in a sauce pan. Heat on high just until a soft boil is reached. Turn heat to medium-low and simmer until liquid is half the amount you started with.

Example: Begin with 3 cups lactose-free milk. Heat and simmer until reduced to 1½ cups.

Using a powdered milk base:

Use 1 cup of powdered milk alternative or a non-dairy creamer. Add ½ cup of water, soymilk, coconut, almond, rice, or lactose-free milk. Using a blender, mix the powder with liquid; set aside for 30 minutes to thicken. Use in any recipe which calls for evaporated canned milk.

BUTTERMILK SUBSTITUTIONS

Using lactose-free, coconut, or soymilk:

For every 1 cup of lactose-free milk, soymilk, almond milk, rice milk, or coconut milk, add:

> 1 tablespoon fresh lemon juice or
> 1 tablespoon white vinegar

Place the milk in a measuring cup. Add lemon or vinegar. Stir until mixed; let sit for 10 minutes. Use this in your recipe as you would buttermilk.

MILK SUBSTITUTIONS

- Soymilk
- Coconut milk (not coconut water)
- Rice milk
- Oat milk
- Lactose-free milk
- Almond milk
- Non-dairy coffee creamer (check label)
- In the place of yogurt or cream cheese:

Most all health food markets and some grocery stores offer a variety of dairy-free products. I've even tried a few very nice faux (tofu based) cream cheese options.

EGG ALTERNATIVES FOR BAKING

For people who would like vegan options when baking or for those who don't mind eggs, but would like to lower the cholesterol content in their recipes, I have included a simple guide for egg substitutions.

FLAX OR CHIA SEED EGG REPLACER

Makes one egg

- 1 tablespoon chia or flaxseed, grounded
- 3 tablespoons hot water

Mix the seed with hot water in a blender, or with a whisk or fork, for 1 to 2 minutes, or until the mixture resembles a gelatin or egg white-like consistency. Use immediately or refrigerate for up 2 weeks.

POWDERED EGG REPLACER

Makes the equivalent of 20 to 25 eggs

- 1¼ cups potato starch
- ¾ cup tapioca starch
- ⅓ cup baking powder
- 2½ tablespoons baking soda

Combine all ingredients and place in an airtight container; store in the refrigerator.

To substitute for 1 egg, use ½ tablespoon of egg replacer powder and 2 tablespoons of water.

CHOLESTEROL LOWERING OPTIONS CONTAINING EGGS

When using the egg substitutes purchased at your local grocery market, follow package instructions. Otherwise, try any one of my homemade alternatives.

Generally; ¼ cup egg mixture = 1 large egg

WHOLE EGG SUBSTITUTE #1

- 6 egg whites
- ¼ cup nonfat dry milk
- 1 tablespoon Extra Virgin Olive Oil

Mix all of the ingredients together until very well blended. May be frozen or stored in the refrigerator for up to 1 week.

WHOLE EGG SUBSTITUTE #2

- 3 egg whites
- ¼ cup of low-fat milk
- 1 tablespoon dry milk powder
- 1 tablespoon Extra Virgin Olive Oil

Beat egg whites lightly with a fork in a small bowl. Add the milk, powdered milk and Olive Oil; beat all the ingredients until thoroughly blended. Cover and refrigerate.

WHOLE EGG SUBSTITUTE #3 (LACTOSE-FREE)

- 3 egg whites
- ¼ cup plain soymilk or lactose-free milk
- 1 tablespoon ground flax seeds
- 1 tablespoon Extra Virgin Olive Oil (pure or light are fine as well)

Mix all of the ingredients together until very well blended. May be stored in the refrigerator for up to 1 week.

ESSENTIAL OILS—GRAS LIST

FDA's common names for Essential Oils Generally Recognized As Safe (GRAS). For a more information about GRAS Essential Oils you may visit www.fda.gov.

Alfalfa	Capsicum	Cola	Glycyrrhiza	**Lime**	**Orange**	Savory
Allspice	Caraway	**Coriander**	Glycyrrhizin	Linden	**Origanum**	Schinus
Almond	Cardamom	Corn	**Grapefruit**	Locust	Palmarosa	Sloe
Ambrette	Carob	Cumin	Guava	Lupulin	Paprika	Spearmint
Angelica	Carrot	Curacao	Hickory	Mace	**Pepper**	Spike
Angostura	Cascarilla	Cusparia	Horehound	Malt	**Peppermint**	Tamarind
Anise	**Cassia**	Dandelion	Hops	**Mandarin**	Peruvian	**Tangerine**
Asafetida	Celery Cherry	Dill	Horsemint	**Marjoram**	Petitgrain	Tannic
Balm	Chervil	Dog	Hyssop	Mate	Pimenta	Tarragon
Balsam	Chicory	Elder	Immortelle	**Melissa**	Pipsissewa	**Thyme**
Basil	**Cinnamon**	Estragole	Jasmine	Menthol	Pomegranate	**Tea Tree**
Bay	Citronella	Estragon	Juniper	Menthyl	Prickly Ash	Triticum
Bergamot	Citrus	**Fennel**	Kola	Molasses	Rose	Tuberose
Bitter	**Clary Sage**	Fenugreek	Laurel	Mustard	**Rosemary**	Turmeric
Bois	**Clove**	Galanga	**Lavender**	Naringin	Rue	Vanilla
Cacao	Clover	Garlic	Lavandin	Neroli	Saffron	Violet
Camomile	Coca	**Geranium**	**Lemon**	Nutmeg	Sage	Ylang-ylang
Cananga	Coffee	**Ginger**	Licorice	Onion	St John's	Zedoary

Although Essential Oils can have amazing medicinal benefits, they are not approved by the FDA to replace any medicine you may be using to treat an illness. Always consult with your physician before using Essential Oils internally or externally as they may conflict with a medicine for which you are currently prescribed.

THERAPEUTIC BENEFITS OF ESSENTIAL OILS REFERENCES

1. http://www.umm.edu/altmed/articles/aromatherapy-000347. htm#ixzz23GzSGBUn

2. Aridoğan BC, Baydar H, Kaya S, et al.: Antimicrobial activity and chemical composition of some essential oils. Arch Pharm Res 25 (6): 860-4, 2002.

3. Singh, G.; Kapoor, I. P. S.; Pandey, S. K.; Singh, U. K.; Singh, R. K. (2002). "Studies on essential oils: Part 10; Antibacterial activity of volatile oils of some spices". Phytotherapy Research 16 (7): 680–2. doi:10.1002/ptr.951, PMID 12410554.

4. D'Auria FD, Tecca M, Strippoli V, et al.: Antifungal activity of Lavandula angustifolia essential oil against Candida albicans yeast and mycelial form. Med Mycol 43 (5): 391-6, 2005.

5. http://www.eductationscotland.gov.uk, Essential_Oils_tcm4-670458.ppt

6. Minami M, Kita M, Nakaya T, et al.: The inhibitory effect of essential oils on herpes simplex virus type-1 replication in vitro. Microbiol Immunol 47 (9): 681-4, 2003.

7. Buchbauer G, Jirovetz L, Jäger W, et al.: Fragrance compounds and essentialoils with sedative effects upon inhalation. J Pharm Sci 82 (6): 660-4, 1993.

8. Ibid

ADDITIONAL STUDIES ON ESSENTIAL OILS

- Aloisi AM, Ceccarelli I, Masi F, et al.: Effects of the essential oil from citrus lemon in male and female rats exposed to a persistent painful stimulation. Behav Brain Res 136 (1): 127-35, 2002.

- Jahangeer AC, Mellier D, Caston J: Influence of olfactory stimulation on nociceptive behavior in mice. Physiol Behav 62 (2): 359-66, 1997.

- Shibata H, Fujiwara R, Iwamoto M, et al.: Immunological and behavioral effects of fragrance in mice. Int J Neurosci 57 (1-2): 151-9, 1991.

- Fujiwara R, Komori T, Noda Y, et al.: Effects of a long-term inhalation of fragrances on the stress-induced immunosuppression in mice Neuroimmunomodulation 5 (6): 318-22, 1998 Nov-Dec.

HEALTH BENEFITS OF OLIVE OIL REFERENCES

1. Penny Kris-Etherton, PhD, RD; Robert H. Eckel, MD; Barbara V. Howard, PhD, Sachiko St. Jeor, PhD, RD; Terry L. Bazzarre, PhD, "Lyon Diet Heart Study: Benefits of a Mediterranean-Style, National Cholesterol Education Program/American Heart Association Step 1 Dietary Pattern on Cardiovascular Disease", 2001, http://circ.ahajournals.org/cgi/content/full/103/13/1823, (22 February 2007).

2. Amy Murphy, "Blood vessels appear healthier after people consume olive oil high in phenolic compounds", 11 November 2005, http://www.medicalnewstoday.com/medicalnews. php?newsid=33381, (22 February 2007).

3. "FDA Allows Qualified Health Claim to Decrease Risk of Coronary Heart Disease", 1 November 2004, http://www.fda.gov/bbs/topics/news/2004/NEW01129.html, (22 February 2007).

4. "Olive Oil reduces blood pressure", 4 November 2004, http://www.nutraingredients.com/news/news-NG.asp?n=55854-olive-oil-reduces, (22 February 2007).

5. "Olive oil linked to lower blood pressure", 8 January 2007, http://www.nutraingredients-usa.com/news/ng.asp?id=73151-olive-oil-mediterranean-diet-blood-pressure, (22 February 2007).

6. L. Aldo Ferrara, MD; A. Sonia Raimondi, MD; Lucia d'Episcopo, RD; Luci Guida, MD; Antonia Dello Russo, MS; Teodoro Marotta, MD, PhD, "Olive Oil and Reduced Need for Antihypertensive Medications", 27 March 2000, http://archinte.ama-assn.org/cgi/content/abstract/160/6/837, (23 February 2007).

7. María-Isabel Covas, MSc, PhD; Kristiina Nyyssönen, MSc, PhD; Henrik E. Poulsen, MD, PhD; Jari Kaikkonen, MSc, PhD; Hans-Joachim F. Zunft, MD, PhD; Holger Kiesewetter, MD, PhD; Antonio Gaddi, MD, PhD; Rafael de la Torre, MSc, PhD; Jaakko Mursu, MSc; Hans Bäumler, MSc, PhD; Simona Nascetti, MD, PhD; Jukka T. Salonen, MD, PhD; Montserrat Fitó, MD, PhD; Jyrki Virtanen, MSc; Jaume Marrugat, MD, PhD, "The Effect of Polyphenols in Olive Oil on Heart Disease Risk Factors", 5 September 2006, http://www.annals.org/cgi/content/abstract/145/5/333#FN, (23 February 2007).

8. "Why does Mediterranean diet protect women from breast cancer? It's in the olive oil", 10 January 2005, http://www.medicalnewstoday.com/medicalnews.php?newsid=18751, (23 February 2007). J.A. Menendez, L. Vellon, R. Colomer, & R. Lupu, "Oleic acid, the main monounsaturated fatty acid of olive oil, suppresses Her-2/neu (erb B-2) expression and synergistically enhances the growth inhibitory effects of trastuzumab (Herceptin™) in breast cancer cells with Her-2/neu oncogene amplification", 10 January 2005, http://annonc.oxfordjournals.org/cgi/reprint/mdi090v1.pdf, (23 February 2007).

9. Roberto Fabiani, Angelo De Bartolomeo, Patrizia Rosignoli, Maurizio Servili, Roberto Selvaggini, Gian Francesco Montedoro, Cristina Di Saverio and Guido Morozzi, March 2006, "Virgin Olive Oil Phenols Inhibit Proliferation of Human Promyelocytic Leukemia Cells (HL60) by Inducing Apoptosis and Differentiation", http://jn.nutrition.org/cgi/content/abstract/136/3/614, (23 February 2007).

10. "Prevent Cancer, Use Olive Oil: New Year's Resolution No. 1", 24 December 2006, http://www.medicalnewstoday.com/medicalnews.php?newsid=58759, (23 February 2007). Anja Machowetz, Henrik E. Poulsen, Sindy Gruendel, Allan Weimann, Montserrat Fitó, Jaume Marrugat, Rafael de la Torre, Jukka T. Salonen, Kristiina Nyyssönen, Jaakko Mursu, Simona Nascetti, Antonio Gaddi, Holger Kiesewetter, Hans Bäumler, Hany Selmi, Jari Kaikkonen, Hans-Joachim F. Zunft, Maria-Isabel Covas and Corinna Koebnick, "Effect of olive oils on biomarkers of oxidative DNA stress in Northern and Southern Europeans" January 2007, http://www.fasebj.org/cgi/content/abstract/21/1/45, (23 February 2007).

11. L Sköldstam, L Hagfors, G Johansson, "An experimental study of a Mediterranean diet intervention for patients with rheumatoid arthritis", 28 June 2002, http://ard.bmj.com/cgi/content/full/62/3/208, (22 February 2007).

Laughter is brightest in the place where food is. ~ Irish Proverb

MICKI SANNAR
ABOUT THE AUTHOR

Want to know more about the best Essential and Olive Oils?

Find Micki: www.facebook.com/aromaoliveoil
Follow Micki: @oliveoilchic
Contact Micki: micki@aromaandoliveoil.com
Visit Micki: www.aromaandoliveoil.com
                www.oliveoildesserts.com

Olive Oil queen Micki Sannar, is all about using healthy oils to create flavor magic. When her family faced pressing health concerns, she had no idea that her desire to bake desserts using only Olive Oil rather than shortening or butter would turn into a culinary innovation and global intrigue. A tiny person packed with as much flair, flavor, and fun as her recipes, her unique and surprising global creations are sure to wow the taste buds and comfort the soul, while bringing simple gourmet into the home kitchen.

Right out of the gate her book, *Olive Oil Desserts: Delicious and Healthy Heart Smart Baking*, was a huge success. It won multiple cooking awards and was featured on Amazon as a "mover and shaker" in the industry. Her next original cook book, *Aroma & Olive Oil* (released September 2012) will be sure to please as she introduces the harmonious blending of olive oil and CPTG Essential Oils, taking cooking to new therapeutic heights.

With more than 25 years of experience, Micki is a sought after local and national cooking celebrity, instructor, and cooking competition judge. She has whipped up her scrumptious concoctions on numerous stages including the National Dessert Convention, QVC's in house kitchen, and Utah's Home and Garden Show. Micki is a happily married mother of 4. She enjoys boating, camping, snorkeling, wave running, writing recipes, reading (especially cookbooks), and spoiling her friends and family with late night treats. It's always a party when Micki is around.

INDEX